JUST SHOOT ME!

A practical guide for using your video camera in youth ministry

JUST SHOOT ME!

A practical guide for using your video camera in youth ministry

Jay Delp and Joel Lusz

Youth Specialties

WWW.ZONDERVAN.COM

Just Shoot Me!: A practical guide for using your video camera in youth ministry

Copyright © 2002 by Youth Specialties

Youth Specialties Books, 300 S. Pierce St., El Cajon, CA 92020, are published by
Zondervan Publishing House, 5300 Patterson Ave. S.E., Grand Rapids, MI 49530.

Library of Congress Cataloging-in-Publication Data
Delp, Jay, 1960-
   Just shoot me! : a practical guide for using your video camera in youth ministry /
Jay Delp and Joel Lusz.
    p. cm.
   ISBN 0-310-23819-6
   1. Church group work with youth—Audio-visual aids. 2. Video recording in church
work. I. Lusz, Joel, 1958- II. Title.

BV4447 .D43 2002
259'.23'0208—dc21

200104683

Web site addresses listed in this book were current at the time of publication. Please
contact Youth Specialties via e-mail (YS@YouthSpecialties.com) to report URLs that
are no longer operational and replacement URLs if available.

Edited by Tim McLaughlin and Dave Urbanski
Cover and interior design by Unidea

Printed in the United States of America

02 03 04 05 06 07 / / 10 9 8 7 6 5 4 3 2 1

Dedications & Acknowledgements

To my amazing mother, Sarah, the most godly woman I know, and the loving memory of my incredibly inventive father, Rowan.

To my sisters, Charlene, Carrie, and Katrina for their lifelong encouragement, friendship, and laughter which enrich my life immeasurably.

—Jay Delp

This book is dedicated to an amazing group of people who have loved me, shared great memories with me, mentored me, challenged me, cared for me, laughed with me and helped to shape me into the Christian man that I am today.

First, to the five most important women in my life: To my mother, Phyllis Lusz Ring, who taught me so much but mostly taught me what it means to love. To my sister, Tracie Runge, who has been my good friend and has always been willing to do whatever it takes to keep our friendship growing. To my mother-in-law, Jewel Patton, who has always supported me, cared for me, loved me, and been the most incredible "Gramma" in the world. To my daughter, Koral, who is the greatest gift I've ever received and whom I love more and more with each passing moment. And finally, to my wife, Angie, whom I love very much and who has been simply wonderful!

Second, to three men who have modeled for me at a deep level what it means to be a Christian man, father, and husband: My dad, Jack Lusz, the most loving and selfless person I've ever known; Dr. Joseph Warner, the most open, honest, and transparent friend I have; and Roland Coffey, the man God gave me to be my father when I was still a teenager. I love and thank you all.

Third, to my best friends: Joe Coffey, Brian Coffey, Scot Houck, Scott "Moose" Timmons, Paul Staup, Ed Pettus, Mike Renfro, Mike Dixon, Jason Ellis, and TJ Young.

And finally, to all the youth I have ever had the privilege to minister with, especially those at my present church, Suntree United Methodist.

—Joel Lusz

103326

CONTENTS

6. Editing: Cookin' Up All That Raw Footage   65

Editing is where the power is...Two ways to edit video...Tape-to-tape (or linear) editing... Computer-based (digital) editing or "Look Ma! No tape!"...
Basic editing tips and techniques...When you must shoot 'n' show

7. Showtime! Putting Your Best Footage Forward   83

Intro to video projectors...How to buy a video projector...The 10 showtime commandments...Front or rear projection?

8. Getting Connected: Born to Be Wired   95

Four video interconnectivity principles...All you need to know about cables...The four most common video hook-ups (or *configurations*, for you sophisticated types)

9. Goin' Live to the Big Screen   105

Basic equipment you need...Some benefits of going live

10. Improving Your Servo (*Servomechanism*, That Is)   109

56 tips for producing better video in youth ministry (or anywhere else, for that matter)

VIDEO IDEAS GALORE!
A Plethora of Projects & Possibilities

Quiet on the Set!

"Step 1. Push the button marked POWER."

That's probably the first thing you read (and rightfully ignored) in your camcorder's user's manual when you first got it. But think of it this way: *Video technology is youth ministry's "power button" that, when pressed, really does turn up the power in some truly remarkable ways.*

- The power to communicate with and through teenagers
- The power to connect with youths
- The power to captivate students' attention
- The power to impact young lives with Gods eternal truth
- The power to build bridges to previously unreached groups of teenagers
- The power to engage and involve adults as well as children and youths
- The power to empower students to tell their stories (or any story) the way they want to tell it
- The power to involve adults in youth ministry
- The power to drain your budget (unfortunately)

Consider this book your video-in-youth-ministry owner's manual. The first section—Using Video in Youth Ministry—helps define exactly what we're talking about. The second section—

Equipping the Saints—is all about technology, tips, and techniques, from the camcorder itself, to a primer on editing, to making your showing a wild success (plus a lot more). The third section—Video Ideas Galore!—is a collection of (you guessed it!) video ideas you can put to use immediately.

On every page, we've kept the discussion pointed to *youth*

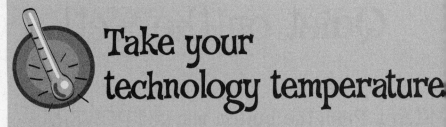

Take your technology temperature

Complete this modest questionnaire to determine just how video-friendly you and your youth ministry are today.

1. *VCR* stands for: (10 pts.)
   a. Very Christian Recording
   b. Video Cassette Recorder
   c. Vivian C. Rosenblum
   d. Victorious Charismatic Response
   e. None of the above

2. Our church/youth ministry owns the following equipment. (check all that apply, 10 pts. for each)
   ___ A TV (must be color, at least 20" in diameter, and manufactured after 1974)
   ___ A VCR
   ___ A video projector (must weigh less than 219 lbs., be smaller than a subcompact imported sports car, and have an image bright enough to use outside of a cave)
   ___ A video camera (or *camcorder*, or *vidcam*; whatever you call it, it must *not* be the two-piece, pre-1987 variety consisting of a portable boat-anchor-like VCR connected to the camera with an umbilical cord)
   ___ A computer (must be newer than a 286 MHz with 64k of RAM; Commodore 64s don't count)

group-oriented video—videos made, edited, and played either *by* teenagers in a youth group or *for* them. And you'll quickly see how much more effective the former is than the latter. We've found that training a cadre of teenagers in videography has immense ministry potential.

3. Define the following: (10 pts. for each correct answer)
   a. Graphics—
   b. Lumens—(hint: it has nothing to do with cough drops)
   c. Strobe—
   d. 8 track—
   e. Disco—

4. We are currently using video in our ministry to: (circle all that apply)
   a. Play *Gilligan's Island* reruns for confirmation class discussion starters (10 pts.)
   b. Produce youth group event highlight tapes (50 pts.)
   c. Critique (or roast) the pastor's sermon during football halftime shows (20 pts.)
   d. Introduce my lesson topic or trigger a discussion on that topic using homegrown video programs (50 pts.)
   e. You mean there are ways to use video in ministry?! (0 pts.)

5. My present attitude towards this whole "video in youth ministry" idea is:
   a. Amen, brother! (addicted video user, probably a pusher, 60 pts.)
   b. Extremely interested (but show me the money: wealth of interest with no wealth, 50 pts.)
   c. Firm believer (40 pts.)
   d. Curious but uncommitted (desperately seeking Sony, 30 pts.)
   e. Skeptic/cynic ("Yeah, right, like I'll ever have the time or money to use video in youth ministry"—digital backslider, 20 pts.)
   f. Video?...uh, what did you say "VCR" stood for again? (Unplugged; the cords attached, but no LCDs are lit up, 10 pts.)
   g. Technology is satanic (0 pts.)

Okay, now score yourself:
200-270 = On board, in touch, cutting edge or close to it
140-199 = Well on your way, but room for improvement
80-139 = Forgive them, for they know not what they do
0 - 79 = You bought this book just in time.

Five fundamental tips for youth group vidcamming

Use lots of props, costumes, and gadgets.

These add to the genuineness and legitimacy of the product. So try to put a lot of appropriate materials into your sketch. If you're doing a spoof on an Old West saloon encounter, for example, give the characters cowboy hats, boots, holsters, fake mustaches—and scatter some hay on the ground. Make the scene believable. In fact, if you're lucky enough to have a basement room where you can store the stuff, start stocking up on video props now. You'll use them!

The ideas that follow aren't sacred—so adapt them to fit you and your group.

Just because the video idea "Pie in the Face" suggests throwing a pie in your senior pastor's face, that doesn't mean it's appropriate material *for you*. (Maybe your group should pie the music director instead!) Just be sure to filter the ideas here through your own sense of what works for your church or group and what doesn't. What's funny to one group may not be funny to another.

And don't stop at making it merely appropriate for you, but take our suggested material and go crazy with it! Add to it! Go overboard! If the idea asks you to "interview parents and ask them to describe their child's eating habits" ("Mr./Ms. Curious with Your Parents," page 150; "Parent Interviews," page 141), go ahead and ask *seven* parents the question—or ask them more questions along that line. Do whatever you want to the basic ideas offered here.

Keep your eyes open.

We get a lot of our ideas from watching TV programs, commercials, kids at school, families interacting, movies, et cetera. Just observe and be aware of what's happening around you, and soon you'll have plenty of homegrown video ideas for your group!

Silly, stupid, and ridiculous are good.

Many have been the times we've begun a video project thinking, *This is sooo stupid*, then in the end, really liking the idea. (Maybe it was still stupid, but it accomplished a worthwhile purpose among its creators and audience.) We've learned that our dumbest, most ridiculous ideas can be our best. So don't dismiss a goofy idea—it just might turn out to be a great one!

And last, manage your time and reduce the stress!

Don't wait 'til the last minute to make a video. It can be time-consuming and stressful in the *best* of circumstances, and trying to rush through the process is a veritable nightmare. Don't even think about making a video the same day you need it. Plan your videos ahead so you're not run ragged at the last minute. This way you'll keep the process fun instead of tense cramming to finish a project.

What this book won't do

- Turn you into the next Steven Spielberg (or George Lucas, or Alfred Hitchcock, or Oliver Stone, or James Cameron, or Uncle Leroy...).
- Earn you an honorary degree in advanced video engineering.
- Cover topics exhaustively. There are other books for that. This book is for in-the-trenches youth workers—not network television-producer-have-my-people-call-your-people youth workers.
- Suggest a particular model camcorder to buy (or any other piece of gear), since by the time you read these words, any model we'd suggest would already be about as state-of-the-art as a T-Rex (that's the extinct carnivorous reptile, not a model of camcorder). Twelve months in the world of electronics is like dog years on steroids.

What this book will do

- Introduce you to vital video issues you need to consider as you develop your use of video in youth ministry in whatever areas and to whatever level is right for you and your kids.
- Help you communicate (at least semi-intelligently) with just about anyone (assuming they speak English or another language you snoozed a few semesters through) about basic video gear and video techniques and technologies.
- Help you avoid common mistakes committed when using video in youth ministry.
- Motivate you to begin or continue using the video medium to accomplish all sorts of purposes in teens' lives—spiritual, social, emotional, aesthetic, or career.
- Stimulate in you ideas and applications especially and specifically suited to your youths and youth ministry.
- Make you want to spend your entire youth ministry budget in one Circuit City shopping spree (that was a joke...don't max out your plastic yet!).

A word to the electronically challenged

Fear not—we bring good tidings to all youth workers who shrink from all things electronic and digital, and especially video: *This is youth ministry, not Twentieth Century Fox.* We know that. And we want you to know that we know that. So don't let technophobia keep you from tapping into the incredible power of using video in youth ministry.

Besides, you may not be the one using the video gadgetry anyway—because a big goal of this book is to *get your students using video* in your ministry. We made this book to be helpful no matter how experienced you are or aren't in video. Some of you lie in bed at night dreaming of owning a professional camera or two with a complete computer-based editing suite that automatically unfolds from behind a rotating bookcase inside your church office. Others of you will be content with just getting your hands (or your students' hands) on a basic camera and few pieces of used video editing gear—gear that can serve you and your specific needs for the next several years and beyond.

So don't feel pressured to make yours a video-centered youth ministry (which is actually a silly idea) or to go out right now and buy top-end gear. Open this book to a chapter that sounds interesting to you, and take it from there. And remember: the goal is not to have you do all the video stuff, but to get teenagers and other adults involved in putting this great medium to work. Let your focus be the state of the heart, not of the art.

USING VIDEO IN YOUTH MINISTRY

What It Means, What It Doesn't

1

Just What Do You Mean By "Using Video in Youth Ministry," and Why Do You Want to Use It?

The four digital laws

First of all, let's make it abundantly clear that we do *not* believe in the Four Digital Laws.

Law 1: Youth workers love teenagers and have wonderful plans for their lives.

Law 2: Youth workers are older and separated from teenagers. Therefore they cannot know and communicate with them.

Law 3: Video technology is God's only provision for youth workers' separation from teenagers. Only through video technology can youth workers know, communicate with, and impact teenagers.

Law 4: We must individually buy and use video technology in our youth ministry if we hope to know and communicate with teenagers.

We just don't buy this. (Well, except maybe for the fourth law, which we think holds *some* truth.) It is not true that *every* youth worker, *every* youth ministry must use video. Far from it—you don't have to use video in your ministry at all. To the contrary, you can be very effective without it. Then again, using video just might move your ministry into a realm of effectiveness you haven't yet experienced with your youth group.

A defining moment

So what do we mean by "using video in youth ministry," anyway? For most youth workers it means playing back prerecorded clips (on rented or purchased videocassettes) of any length or quality (in any youth ministry setting for any purpose).

You're reading this because you're obviously looking for an entirely different, more active use of video. So what do you think of this definition?

Using video in youth ministry is applying the skills and technology for capturing, preparing, and presenting video images to any or all goals, tasks, or purposes of youth ministry.

This will be our working definition in this book.

The two worlds of using video in youth ministry

Here's what we see as the two worlds of video use in youth groups:

Simply put, this means that every image is either—
- A live image coming directly from a camera, or
- A prerecorded image played back from a VCR, camcorder, DVD, computer hard drive, or other technologies that will continue to emerge.

You may already be applying ideas from both worlds in your ministry. For example, have you ever used a video camera, video projector, and screen to project an enlarged, live image of what was simultaneously taking place on the stage or platform? A great idea for concerts, youth rallies and conferences, and worship services of all flavors.

On the other hand, any time you pop a videotape into a VCR or even playback video clips from a computer or DVD, you are in playback world (since the images aren't live, but rather prerecorded and played back from some device designed for playback of video images).

But wait! There's more! Any video production you show in youth ministry—that is, a playback video—or anywhere else for that matter, will be either homegrown or prefab.
- Homegrown videos are productions you make yourself— you didn't buy it, rent it, or borrow the program. You shot it with a video camera of some kind, maybe you edited it (more about this in chapter six), and played it for your entire youth-group world to see.
- Prefab videos—these you bought, borrowed, or rented. This is the world most youth workers are well acquainted with.

Both worlds are great places. Both have tons to offer to your youth ministry. Yet we believe (because we've experienced this first-hand) that homegrown videos represent greater

The two worlds
of using video
in youth ministry

"LIVE" World

"PLAYBACK" World

"Pre-Fab" World

"Home-Made" World

The sub-worlds
of Playback World

potential and possibilities for youth groups—greater capability to build bridges to teenagers and their faith development.

This entire book is focused on the wonderfully exciting, creatively limitless, and powerfully personal world of homegrown videos. Here's why we're a little biased about the superiority (usually) of homegrown videos over prefab videos:

• Where can you buy, rent, or borrow Christian video programming that stars the kids in your very own youth group?
• Which is more personal, homegrown or prefab?
• If done well, which will your students want to show their friends and family—homegrown or prefab?
  Which will your students be more interested in—the latest million-dollar, broadcast-quality program produced by Hollywood, or your rough-around-the-edges, $37.39 "feature" guest starring Ashley (your silent sophomore) or Justin (a Robin Williams wannabe) or Julie (the homecoming queen)?

Do the math:

YOUTH WORKER + STUDENTS + VIDEO GEAR = MANY MAGNIFICENT MINISTRY MOMENTS

Hey, don't misunderstand us. Prefab videos are a tremendous blessing and resource you should take advantage of. There are some killer video tools out there produced by some of the most creative minds in the Christian world—videos you can use effectively in nearly all aspects of youth ministry. All we're saying is that we're a couple of vidiots convinced that youth workers can and should be using video in outrageously creative ways with the students God has called them to minister to.

Finally, a big premise in this book is involving youths in the process of creating video—mainly because the ministry potential in involving your students in creating homegrown videos is unlimited (unlike your budget).

The top 10 reasons for using video in youth ministry

You've got a ministry.
You've got a camcorder.
Insert the latter into the former.

10. Video is a powerful audiovisual medium for an audiovisual culture.

If we grew up in the 1950s or later, we were nursed on the networks, cradled by cable, tutored with television, and captivated by camcorders. We have been increasingly and more deeply trained to pay attention to what comes into our world through images, instead of by the printed or spoken word. We can deny it, decry it, or despise it, but this A/V reality will only accelerate in the coming years. The idea isn't *If you can't beat 'em, join 'em,* but rather *Beat 'em at their own game,* or better yet, *Use their medium for God's message and purposes.*

9. Video is the language of today's generation.

And they speak it fluently. This became glaringly obvious to Jay when he sat down to edit a video with a bunch of middle schoolers—before long he was just pushing buttons at the direction of the undersized, unchurched kids. They intuitively knew what worked and what didn't work—knew exactly when they wanted to cut each scene in and out, knew they wanted every clip in black and white, knew the precise title, font, color of every title (once he demonstrated a few of the possibilities), and knew the music they wanted for each segment.

Not that the students couldn't learn a few things about creating video. But it demonstrates what you've probably seen, too they know how to speak the language of video even if they don't know what buttons to push. (The first step in ministering to any unfamiliar culture, whether in New Guinea or New Jersey, is to learn and use the native language.)

5. Video has widespread acceptance and even fascination.

Not merely when youths are being videotaped, but much more when they are operating the camcorder and other video gear themselves. Offer the camera to one of those kids who runs and hides when a camera is pointed at her—and suddenly she will become a willing participant, if not a producer or director, in the video production.

6. Homegrown video has unlimited creative, relevant, and personal possibilities.

Pick a topic, any topic—or Bible text—and there are dozens and dozens of effective videos just waiting to happen that you and your students can produce (and that meet all three criteria: creative, relevant, and personal). In fact, if all your students created videos on the same topic or Bible text, the resulting productions would all be different—because your students each bring individual and unique insights, perspectives, and tastes to the production process.

7. Video can build bridges into teens' lives.

Creating a homegrown video connects adults with teenagers who are otherwise resistant (at best) and unreachable (at worst).

Jay remembers a birthday party he said he'd chaperone for a friend's 7th-grade son and his five friends. What to do with six highly animated pubescent males for three hours in a restaurant's curtained-off banquet room? So Jay packed his video camera, portable video light, a small TV/monitor, and some other supplies, and headed out to face the lions.

It didn't take him long to figure out these guys were into inline skating and skateboarding. In fact, they had brought their skates and boards along. After dispensing with the pizza-and-cake rituals, they all headed out to the parking lot to skate, bending their collective imaginations to all variety of inappropriate ways to spend the next two hours.

So out comes Jay's camcorder and TV—which produces instant, fierce desires among the guys to be either Jim Carrey or George Lucas. The least proficient skater had just the excuse he needed for not skating—"I needed a camera operator." For the next two hours, the boys' innovative production ideas were as numerous as Jay's silent prayers on behalf of his $800 camera that the overzealous camera operator handled with toylike recklessness.

Then came the payoff. "Hey," one of them yelled to Jay, "can you come and videotape me and my friends at the skate park tomorrow night?" Jay had known this kid precisely two hours, he was three times the kid's age, and yet he had just received an invitation into the skate rat's world. We've seen this bridge-building power of video over and over again in our ministry with teenagers.

5. Video gives students the power to create and communicate.

For most of their young lives, they've been spectators at adult-produced programs, whether at church or on cable—programs designed by adults, shot by adults, edited by adults, written, produced, and directed by adults, and presented by adults. Thousands of programs, thousands of hours.

Now you come along and say, "Wanna make your own production? Wanna tell your own story the way you want to tell it? Here are the tools and training to do it. It's pretty easy."

Seldom have youths been trusted by any adult for this kind of opportunity, this kind of control. By providing teenagers access to their language (video), the resources for creating their own messages with that language (time, tools, and training you provide for them), and your affirmation, encouragement, and support, you have equipped your students to involve themselves like never before in the church. Give 'em the power, and set 'em loose!

4. Video technology is available to all of us.

This has been true for only the last several years. And with the ever-decreasing cost of "desktop video" and the ever-increasing number of tools available, it's becoming impossible to say,

'Well, maybe others can add video to their youth ministry, but I can't." Desire, commitment, creativity, and persistence are vital qualities on your digital journey—so don't talk yourself out of it before you've begun.

3. Video can grant you access to the thoughts, feelings, and opinions of almost anyone.

For some reason, people are much more inclined to offer you their thoughts, feelings, and opinions about subjects they'd ordinarily clam up about if they're talking to a camcorder. Maybe the camera and attending crew give the interviewee a sense of importance, contribution, and power. When handled properly, video clearly gives the interviewer, the camera operator, and the crew power to elicit what they couldn't in private conversations.

2. Video can greatly contribute to every aspect and purpose of youth ministry.

It's difficult to think of a youth ministry component that video can't contribute to in one way or another. Part 3 of this book provides you with specific ideas and projects for just about every aspect of youth ministry. Some are simply for fun and entertainment, others are for faith building and discipleship, still others are for affirmation or encouragement—then there's community building, bridge-building, fundraising, parent relationships...the list goes on.

1. Huh?

This is your top reason for using homegrown video in your ministry. You know your youth group best, so jot down here your number-one reason for involving your kids in creating videos: _____

2

What Using Video in Youth Ministry Is *Not*

A few techno traps to avoid when using video in youth ministry

Using video in youth ministry is not...
• A substitute for good communication skills

Using video in your ministry—whether in your lessons and messages or in your students' projects—won't transform poor communication into good communication. Don't fool yourself into thinking you can slip by with poor communication skills until Y3K because you can dazzle your group with technology. The ability to effectively communicate with students—in speaking/teaching/presenting situations as well as in relating/conversing situations—is vital and cannot be smokescreened by video technology. In fact, use video to improve your speaking by videotaping your messages and then watching them and critiquing yourself. (Yes, it's a painful exercise at first!)

Using video in youth ministry is not...
• A guarantee of ministry success

There are a lot of false barometers for measuring youth ministry success. Let's not add state-of-the-art video system to the list. Sure, we're convinced that involving youths and adults in ministry-based video can be an awesome ingredient in just about anyone's youth group—but it's certainly not written in stone that you'll succeed as a youth worker because you use video. Technology makes a lousy savior. (Besides, we already have one.)

Using video in youth ministry is not...

• A magic cure for systemic ministry problems

If there's division on your student leadership team—and instead of preparing to confront this problem at your next planning session you spend all your time putting together a highlight video of your last event—then it's time to turn off the editing gear. Sure, they'd love that kind of video, and you'd get a jumbo helping of affirmation. But in your heart you'd know it isn't the best way to prepare for your time together. (On the other hand, if you use video in any number of ways to communicate God's vision for unity, vision, and forgiveness in your group, then you may be onto something.)

Using video in youth ministry is not...

• An excuse for keeping up with the church across town

Hey, did you see the sparkling new, just-released, ultra-light, multiformat, nonlinear, rechargeable, digital LCD, optical zoom, infrared-remote-controlled, waterproof, solar-powered, 90-gig, miniature camcorder that Grace Fellowship just got? The Bible is replete with warnings against, as St. Paul put it, "comparing themselves among themselves." That goes double for comparing technology or video productions. Avoid technology snobbery and electronic envy as you would a virus.

Using video in youth ministry is not...

An electronic Band-Aid to cover up poor planning and preparation

Although this applies more to the teaching/speaking aspects of video in youth ministry than to involving youths in video, it's a rap either way. If you find yourself at the video rental shop two Saturday nights a month under the delusion that "I just want to find a short video clip to supplement my lesson," and the clip turns out to be 48 minutes long—you've got a problem. Balance is the key (not, in this case, white balance—see page 50).

Using video in youth ministry is not...

A substitute for vital leadership and character qualities

Video isn't a substitute for anything significant in youth ministry—especially not for leadership and character qualities. As members of this fallen-yet-redeemed human race, we find it hard to shake the urge to camouflage our failures of leadership with all sorts of things—our excellent teaching ministry, our rapport with students, our videographic talents. Don't let your excitement for involving students in using this powerful tool distract you from the need you may have to grow in leadership or work at overcoming this or that character flaw.

EQUIPPING THE SAINTS

Technology, Tips, & Techniques

3

Format Matters
(Uhh...What Again Is a *Format*?)

Square one for using video in youth ministry
is answering video-format questions such as:

- Which format should you choose to videotape in?
- Why should you choose one format over another?
- What are the long-term implications of choosing a particular
  format?
- What format is best for your ministry?
- What format represents the best quality and value for the
  price?

And, of course, although we wince to write it, the question that
determines direction for youth workers everywhere:

What format is cheapest? (Be careful of this one, though! In
video, as in many other fields, what appears to be least expensive often turns out to be very expensive in the long run in
terms of time, wasted programming, frustration, and money.)
   Each format—that is, tape size and specifications—has
advantages and disadvantages. Your needs and preferences

determine what format you should use, so we'll touch on the pros and cons of each format, including related equipment purchases and the picture quality you should expect in your completed video programs.

A very, very brief video history lesson

Score: JVC 1, Sony nada.

Way back in the 20th century—the late 1970s, to be more precise—Sony invented and released the first widely accepted consumer video format, calling it Beta. JVC countered the next year with the release of the now-ubiquitous consumer video format called VHS. The Beta format was technically superior to the VHS and even had a smaller tape shell (smaller format). But VHS won out in the end because JVC sold the rights to its VHS technology to other manufacturers, creating a tidal wave

Some definitions

(so you sound like you know what you're talking about when you go buy a camcorder)

Extended Play (EP)

The lowest-quality recording mode a video recording device is capable of. Also travels under the name of SLP (Super Long Play). Don't use it. At all. Ever. Okay, maybe if you have only one tape on which to record six hours of *The Dukes of Hazzard* reruns.

FireWire

(Also known as IEEE 1394 and i.Link.) The digital connection found on all new digital video cameras. Audio and video are transferred simultaneously through FireWire as digital data so there's no generation loss. It's just like copying a computer floppy disk. Many other devices, both video and computer-related, are being manufactured with FireWire ports built in for instant digital compatibility. FireWire is the standard on most computer-based editing systems, for both consumers and high-end editors.

of VHS equipment—namely, VCRs and cameras—that saturated the market. Sony, in the meantime, clung to its Beta technology like a selfish fourth grader with a new Gameboy. Thus the "format wars" were born and have continued ever since. (Okay. Lesson over!)

Eight formats to choose from

Here's a list of eight video formats with their advantages and shortcomings—formats with the most relevance to the largest number of youth workers. The formats are listed roughly in order of quality from lowest to highest, although the differences between some formats are undetectable and sometimes arguable. Price-wise, they're all within the financial reach of most youth workers or youth ministries that want to put video to work in ministry.

Generation Loss
The loss of picture and sound quality experienced from duplication of the original master video recording. Repeated duplications from a copy of a copy compound generation loss in nondigital duplication. Not an issue when duplicating digital formats using FireWire.

Linear
Analog, tape-based, not digital. Evil (in terms of convenience and quality, not in a moral sense—though sometimes we wonder). Linear editing has to be done in a line, sequentially, whereas nonlinear—or digital—editing can be done out of sequence, in any order.

Resolution
The amount of information on the screen. Usually represented by pairs of numbers, like 240 x 485 or 1280 x 1024. The first number is the horizontal resolution, and the second is the vertical resolution. The higher the numbers, the better the resolution. And the better the image!

Standard Play (SP)
The highest quality recording mode that a video recording device (VCR or camcorder) is capable of. Use it. All the time. Eternally.

VHS (Video Home System; full-size)

Advantages
- Market saturation. Just about everybody has VHS VCRs. Therefore the final video format of nearly every video production includes VHS. However, the Internet and other digital recording media (DVD, etc.) is fast changing this.
- Inexpensive tape stock
- Long recording time (two or more hours in best-quality SP mode; up to eight hours in EP mode)
- Used editing gear (tape-to-tape, linear) available cheap—a big plus for most youth ministry budgets

Shortcomings
- Tied for last (along with 8mm) for the poorest quality video format available today
- Large tape size results in less-than-portable gear
- Significant generation loss
- New, full-size VHS camcorders are becoming extinct, more rare every year
- Shorter shelf life than digital formats

8mm (8 millimeter)

Advantages
- Small tape size
- Small camera size
- Long recording time in SP mode (2 hours)
- Overtook VHS as the most popular camcorder format in the late 1990s, but is being overtaken by miniDV and Digital8.

Shortcomings
- Similar quality to VHS (i.e., not good)
- Significant generation loss
- A bit more expensive tape stock than VHS
- Limited options in tape-to-tape editing gear

VHS-C (Compact VHS)

Advantages
- Small tape size
- Small camera size
- Instant compatibility with full-size VHS VCRs through a playback/recording adapter

Shortcomings
- Picture quality—same as full-size VHS, since it's the exact same tape formulation but in a smaller shell
- Tape stock even more expensive than 8mm and VHS
- Short recording times (20-40 minutes in highest quality SP mode)

Hi8 (High Resolution 8mm–basically, 8mm on steroids)

Advantages
- Picture quality—superior to VHS, VHS-C, and 8mm
- Small tape size
- Small camera size
- Long recording time (2 hrs.) in SP mode (same as regular 8mm)
- Inexpensive used gear available with the release of new digital formats
- High quality audio
- Less generation loss than VHS, 8mm, and VHS-C

Shortcomings
- Picture quality inferior to digital formats (DV, miniDV, Digital8 and so on)
- Even more expensive tape stock than 8mm (regular 8) and VHS
- Not as much traditional editing gear (linear, tape-to-tape), new or used, on the market compared to used VHS gear

- Generation loss still a significant problem
- Improved picture quality can only be realized by using Hi8 gear, which is more expensive than 8mm gear

SVHS (Super VHS–basically, VHS on steroids)

Advantages
- Picture quality—superior to VHS, 8mm, VHS-C
- Wide range of new and used gear available for shooting and editing
- Less generation loss than VHS, 8mm, and VHS-C

Shortcomings
- Picture quality inferior to digital formats (DV, miniDV, Digital8 et cetera)
- Even more expensive tape stock than VHS and 8mm
- Large tape size
- Large camera size
- Generation loss still a significant problem
- This format's improved picture quality can be realized only by using SVHS gear, which is more expensive than VHS gear

SVHS-C (Compact Super VHS)

Advantages
- Small tape size
- Small camera size
- Better picture quality than VHS, 8mm, and VHS-C
- Less generation loss than VHS, 8mm, and VHS-C
- Compatible with full-size SVHS gear (and some VHS) through a playback/recording adapter

Shortcomings
- Expensive tape stock (highest per-minute cost of the eight formats)

- Short recording times (20 to 40 minutes in highest-quality SP mode)
- Generation loss still a significant problem
- Limited and diminishing camera selection—both new and used

Digital8

Advantages
- Good picture quality (significant superiority over all nondigital formats listed so far)
- Digital FireWire connection
- Small tape size
- Small camera size
- High-quality audio
- Gear is upward-compatible with 8mm and Hi8 (you can play and record 8mm and Hi8 tapes on Digital 8 gear, but not vice versa)

Shortcomings
- Picture quality not quite as good as other digital formats (DV, miniDV, and so on), though the difference is only noticeable to professional eyes
- More expensive tape stock than VHS and 8mm
- No "prosumer" (professional consumer), semiprofessional, or professional cameras available when this book went to press
- Cameras are more expensive than nondigital ones

DV, MiniDV (Digital Video)

Advantages
- Best picture quality of any consumer format. Equal to some professional formats when using a high-quality miniDV camera
- Digital FireWire connection
  Smallest tape size

- Long in-camera recording times (60 to 80 minutes in SP, 90 to 120 minutes in LP)
- No generation loss when using FireWire connection to copy footage
- Wide and growing range of gear (consumer, semi-professional, professional)
- Highest resolution and color richness of any consumer format
- New gear available and expanding
- Wide acceptance and market saturation

Shortcomings
- More expensive tape stock than VHS and 8mm
- Cameras are more expensive than nondigital ones
- Incompatible with home VHS VCRs

Our final answer to the format question, if you really want to know

We're continually asked what format we recommend for youth ministry. So we'll tell ya: we definitely, confidently, enthusiastically, highly, strongly, and unapologetically recommend—

MiniDV

—and any other digital format, like Digital 8, DV, DVCam, and DVCPro.

There, we said it. Acquire the FireWire.

Why miniDV, you ask?

- Because of its incredibly improved picture quality over other nondigital formats.
- Because of its conveniently portable honey-I-shrunk-the-format size.
- Because it's instantly compatible and controllable with the myriad of computer-based editing systems you already own (or will own in the not-too-distant-future).
- Because this format has the best price/quality ratio.

- Because the FireWire connection means no generation loss of picture quality.
- Because a steady stream of miniDV gear is being manufactured, and prices are dropping like seventh graders at a lock-in at 4 a.m.

A caveat: You know as well as we do that mere weeks after this book goes to press, someone will introduce an entirely new format that is smaller, better, cheaper, faster (and incompatible with any existing format, of course). That's just the nature of the electronic beast. At the time of this writing there are some tapeless camcorders being experimented with and even introduced—cams that may take the place of miniDV.

Our prophecy from the cheap seats, however, is that miniDV will be around for some time to come in one form or another. (We are fully expecting getting "Gotcha!" letters from some of you in the 2020s, pointing out that you just bought a solar-powered camcorder for $99 that records eight hours of broadcast-quality video on a digital disk the size of a nickel and slips into your portable computer-based editing system, which itself is voice-activated and the size of today's Palm V.)

The wisest advice we can give you is invest in the best format you can afford that accomplishes your goals for using video in youth ministry. Just remember that no matter what format you choose or are stuck with now, you can use all the ideas in the third section of this book—providing you have the video tools necessary to carry out those ideas. The difference between all these formats basically boils down to the price and picture quality of your completed program.

Enough format stuff, already. Let's move on to the video technology tool at the heart of all video in youth ministry—the camcorder.

4

Camcorders
A Room with a Viewfinder

"Is that thing on?"

—most frequently uttered expression by students videotaped by their youth leaders, according to an entirely unscientific survey conducted by the authors

Ah, the camcorder—with it, you'll collect everything you need to cook up your powerfully personal productions, be they frivolous or faith-building. It will accompany you as you stumble onto the chairlift during your ski retreat and as you sweat through a week of semitropical housebuilding in Mexico. Through fundraisers and graduations and conferences, through meetings and events and trips of all kinds, the camcorder will be as constant a companion as you desire. Without the camcorder, there can be no Super Senior Satires production, no Year-in-Review program, no Movie Madness Road Rally—or any of the other outrageously original video ideas you already may have, not to mention those in the final section of this book.

There are features, and then there are *features*

In this chapter we'll look at some video camera features. By the time you're finished with this chapter, you'll be sufficiently conversant in video-ese to impress any unsuspecting salesperson. Chapter 5 offers some advice on how and where to get your hands on a camcorder and other video gear through traditional and not-so-traditional means. Chapter 10 gives you a lifetime supply of tips and techniques for using your camcorder more effectively.

With the proliferation of video cameras, chances are excellent that you're already using one. Today's units are easy to use and getting easier, so we won't waste any time telling you that pushing the button marked POWER turns the power on. Instead let's take a few pages to list and briefly explain some camcorder features—what they are, what they do, why you may want them, and for what it's worth, our opinion about them.

21 camcorder features you should understand

AGC (Automatic Gain Control). An audio feature that automatically adjusts the incoming audio levels to eliminate distortion of loud sounds. You know, like when your group's sophomore pest sneaks up on you and, six inches from your camera's microphone (and a mere 10 inches from your ears), yells, "IN YOUR FACE!" at around 190 decibels. AGC—a good thing considering the sophomore pests in this world.

Audio dub (also called audio insert). An editing feature that allows you to replace an original audio track with music, narration, sound effects (f/x, in shorthand), or any other noise, without disrupting the video image. If you lack access to editing gear, then this feature is helpful to have on your camcorder. Otherwise, it's best left for equipment specifically designed for editing.

Auto focus. Standard on most camcorders. Designed to automatically focus whatever you videotape. Not found on most professional cameras. Good in some situations, less than helpful in many others. Often ends up performing like "automatically out-of-focus," especially when videotaping through glass or a fence. Thankfully, with most camcorders you can override the auto-focus system and use manual focusing for more control and creativity.

Backlight switch. Designed to compensate for the negative effects of videotaping a subject that is between the camera and the light source—window, sun, et cetera. Mildly effective on most units. Best advice: don't shoot into a light source.

CCD (Charge Couple Device) or "chip." The cameras of yester-year had tubes that deteriorated rapidly with age and eventually burned out. All modern video cameras, however, use "chips" (CCDs), which are much more effective for capturing moving video images. All consumer cameras are one-chip cameras. Some "prosumer" and all professional cameras have three chips—a huge improvement in color, clarity, and, you guessed it, price. If you can afford a three-chip camera for any price, go for it. Three chips are much better than one!

Digital zoom. Designed to allow you to reach out and tape someone—even further than manual zoom allows. Some digital zooms are not much good beyond 30x or 40x. Improvements in digital zoom technology now allow useable images captured up to 100x. Many cameras offer some form of digital zoom. Nice feature in most cases.

DVE (Digital Video Effects). Many cameras offer a variety of digital f/x—strobe, mosaic, negative, trails, rasterization, paint, and the like. They're basically eye candy and should be used sparingly while shooting because they're permanent—you can never edit them out later—and because most can be added in editing when so desired. DVE is sure fun to play with, though.

EIS. So what do you think EIS means?
  A. Evangelical Interdenominational Studies
  B. Electronic Image Stabilization
  C. Electronic Ignition System
  D. Extremely Inferior Singer
  Good guess! Electronic Image Stabilization is designed to eliminate minor shakes (not the roller coaster variety) that are practically unavoidable when videotaping without a tripod. Many cameras have it. You can turn it on or off depending whether the type of shooting you're doing calls for it. We recommend this feature.

Frame. In U.S. video standards, a frame is 1/30 of a second. Which means that U.S. videotape systems play at 30 frames per second (fps). In case you're wondering, 16mm film plays at 24 fps.

Gain. Although normally the gain is off, turning up the gain can dramatically improve picture quality in low-light conditions. Many cameras let you set gain in increments, from 0db (normal) to 6db, 9db, 12db, or 18db. The more expensive the camera, the more manual gain settings you'll find. You pay a price for high gain, however: *the higher the gain, the grainier your picture.* Still, the gain control is a marvelous feature that salvages many dark, otherwise unrecordable scenes.

High-speed shutter. Found on many cameras with a variety of shutter speeds ranging from, oh, 1/100 to 1/10,000 of a second, with anywhere from four to seven speeds in between those extremes. Good for taping sports and other fast-action scenes you want to pause or play back in slow motion without the blurs that would normally be found if the film had been shot with normal shutter speeds. The faster the shutter speed, the more light you'll need—so this feature is best used outdoors or in very well-lit indoor settings.

Laser link. Feature on some cameras that allows you to watch your videotape on a TV, wirelessly. Works only on certain TVs. Even compatible TVs need an external receiver, sold separately. Nice little feature, but not vital.

Long shot (a.k.a., wide shot). The camera view of a subject or scene from a distance showing the big picture or broad perspective. The opposite of close-up. Also applies to the likelihood of disco breaking into *Rolling Stone*'s top 20 again, "YMCA" at skating rinks notwithstanding.

Macro. A camera lens feature that lets you videotape objects or even photographs very close to the camera lens. Good feature for videotaping small photographs and other objects from very close up. On many cameras.

Manual zoom. The best zooms are variable speed and increase and decrease the zoom speed depending on the amount of pressure you apply to the zoom control. The zoom control deserves the Most Abused Camcorder Feature Award.

ND (Neutral Density filter). A filter you can mount on the front of the camcorder lens. Professional cameras have this filter built in for easy adjustment. The most important thing to know about an ND filter is that it's great for videotaping in bright sunlight to improve picture quality and color accuracy.

Night vision. Pretty cool feature that actually lets you get a somewhat useable image in total darkness, thanks to infrared technology. The subject being taped must be at fairly close range (10 feet or less).

Resolution. The amount of picture detail reproduced by a video system/format. A camera's resolution is influenced by the chips (CCDs), lens, and recording format. It has nothing to do with what you decide to do on January 1 and ignore by February 1.

Time-lapse recording. Cool feature on some cameras and editing systems that allows you to record a series of very short clips (half a second or less) over a long period of time. We've all seen time-lapse recordings on TV—flowers opening, clouds scudding across the sky, street traffic increasing and thinning out during the course of a day's commute.

Video dub (also called video insert). Does to video what audio dub does to audio. Allows you to replace a portion of your recorded video program with another video clip without disrupting the audio tracks.

White balance. An electronic adjustment on all camcorders (some automatic, some manual, some with both) designed to reproduce true colors so the jerseys on the local Fighting Orangeman are actually orange and not a disgusting green hue.

5

Gettin' in Gear
Questions to Ask, Decisions to Make *before* Spending a Dollar

"Rad."

—the verbatim, profound response of a 12-year-old upon viewing some video footage of him skateboarding, touched up with special effects. (It touched us, too.)

Don't buy yet! Answer these 12 crucial questions first

You've sold too many pizzas, washed too many cars, cooked too many spaghetti dinners, and kidnapped too many members of the pastoral staff for fundraising "ransom" to spend your budget's hard-earned cash without first putting down the video catalog and spending some time dwelling among the 12 forthcoming questions. They could save you much in future fiscal frustration and help point the way for building a ministry through video that's uniquely suited to your passion, purpose, and purse.

Besides, who said you had to spend all that money on *new* equipment? (More on this later in the chapter.)

1. How do you want to use video in youth ministry?

What do you want to do, do better, or do first with video in youth ministry? Do you want the ability to edit video...or edit video better? Do you want to tape youth group events and edit highlight videos of those events? Do you want to start a student production team/ministry with teens taping teens? Do you want to project live video images for youth services and events?

This question is numero uno, The Big One. And its answer spawns as many questions as answers. For example:

• What are your short- and long-term priorities with video?
• What can you do immediately the most effectively?
• What passions and visions do you, your staff, or your students have?
• What, in your ministry setting, has the greatest potential in terms of video usage?

If you simply want to take existing and future video footage and make them "watchable" through editing, then you probably shouldn't go out and buy a new video projector—at least not at first.

If you want to interview freshmen on video so you can send the tape to them when they graduate from high school—and if you don't have a video camera or access to one—then acquiring one now becomes your first priority.

If you want to project song lyrics and announcements for youth services and already have a video camera, then a video projector, computer, and presentation software are your top three priorities.

You get the idea. *First* decide what you want to do, and *then* get the equipment you need to do it.

2. What video equipment do you have access to now?

If your answer is a 8mm silent movie projector, a flannelgraph board with cloth characters from a Noah's Ark lesson, a filmstrip projector, and an eight-track player with two broken track selectors—then your answer to this question is zip, nada, nil. (Psst...actually those 8mm film projectors can still be a lot of fun if you can find a place to develop the film!)

Many churches already have, or soon will have, a decent video projector. If yours doesn't, this could be a great tool to acquire now, not just for youth ministry, but also for use in every ministry of your congregation. No matter what kinds of videos you show in youth ministry, video projectors are the video presentation devices of choice these days. (More on this in chapter seven.)

Do any youth workers on your team, or any students' parents, have camcorders available for taping youth events or whatever it is you want to videotape? Put that to work. Start collecting that raw material which will be fodder for your powerfully personal productions.

Whatever you have or don't have right now, the rule is *make the most of it.* So you don't have that dream gear—yet. What ideas and projects could you do very effectively and creatively now? Do 'em!

3. How will you pay for video equipment?

Once you start talking about using video in youth ministry, it won't take long for your supervisory board of deacons or elders or whoever to ask this question.

Unless someone donates video gear to your ministry, someone or a group of someones will have to pay for the gear—whether it's the youth group with a special fundraiser (just what you need, more fundraisers...) or a local parishioner-owned business. Or maybe the board chairperson will call you tomorrow and say, "Kara, last night the Lord told me in a dream that you have a desire to impact teenagers through video. Then this morning while eating breakfast the number 10,000 kept popping into my head. Does this have any significance to you?"

Don't fret the dollars for now. We'll deal with that later. Just answer this question: *When it comes time to invest in video gear, what is the most probable source or sources of funds to pay for the gear?*

Your answer to this question may affect your answer to the next.

4. Who will be responsible for the equipment?

A control issue, for sure. The youth pastor wants it in his office or house. The senior pastor wants it in the church office, available for many uses. The elders want it in a subterranean vault under lock and key, with one duplicate key—and you get neither key. It may be sticky arriving at an answer, but this is an answer you need before you buy. Once you submit your proposal for obtaining video gear, this issue will inevitably be among the board's questions for you.

5. What human resources/skills are available?

Virtually all congregations, large and small, have at least one student or adult with more than a passing interest in all things audiovisual. Tap into them by tapping 'em on the shoulder and asking them to be part of the church's video ministry. You didn't think you were going to do all this yourself, did you? Sitting within a hundred feet of you every Sunday morning is probably a budding video editor, camera operator, graphic designer, audio engineer, projector technician, voice-over narrator, sound-effects guru, musician, director, set designer, special-effects expert, computer-software geek, lighting technician, or scriptwriter—to name more than a few.

People are what this whole thing is about. Many people have accomplished more than they thought they could because somebody else thought they could. Fan some flames (2 Timothy 1:6) and start asking people, especially students, if they'd be interested being a part of a video-related project if they could choose their favorite area of fascination or expertise.

6. Who will use the equipment?

A close cousin to question 4, but different. You or other adults may ultimately be *responsible* for the equipment, but it's the *students* who may be the primary users. Or perhaps an adult with the vision, time, and skill to contribute to the youth ministry by being involved in helping to edit and produce video programs—while the youth pastor or some other adult oversees the operation and is responsible for the equipment. What you *don't* want is to have video equipment sitting around idle or broken with no one using it or taking responsibility for it.

It's also a good idea to broach the subject of how you will handle requests from individuals and organizations outside your church staff to borrow the equipment. Trust us, it will happen.

7. How much can you invest initially?

If you have 500 bucks to invest initially, then cross off NEW VIDEO PROJECTOR from your video-shopping list. Once you know how much you have to spend, coupled with your answer to question 1 *(What do you want to do with video in youth ministry?)*, you're well on your electronic way to narrowing down your options to the particular video equipment (camera, editor, projector, et cetera) you're in the market for.

8. What format will you use?

Unless you're already committed to a particular format, you'll need to answer this question early in the process. Your answer, of course, depends on your understanding the pros and cons of each format (see page 37) and the reality—not the fantasy—of the picture quality of each format. It's not uncommon for folks to invest in video gear only to experience Visual Depression Syndrome when they see the end result on the big screen—all because they saved a few dollars with a low-end video format and still expected broadcast-quality programs. Choose a format with your eyes wide open. We will say it again: *Invest in the best format you can afford*—hopefully miniDV or better.

9. What will it cost to do what you want to do?

A major variable in your answer is how you will obtain gear (donation, purchase new, purchase used, et cetera), but less obvious are ongoing costs associated with your use of video in youth ministry. Blank tapes cost money, so the dollars you spend on blank tapes each month will be primarily determined by your answers to questions 1 and 8 (*What do you want to do with video, and what format will you use to do it?*). Other recurring expenses include—

- Video-projector bulbs
- Shipping/mailing costs (if you want to ship videotapes to missionaries, objects of community outreach, and so on).
- Duplication costs (unless you duplicate your own tapes)
- Equipment maintenance and repair (who will you call when your video gear ceases to function properly?)
- Insurance (might be a good idea if you invested significantly in equipment. Strings of church robberies are not uncommon, and audio-video equipment goes first.)

10. What training will be provided?

One of Jay's pet ecclesiastical peeves (isn't each believer allotted two?) is this whole practice of calling people to minister, receiving their willing and prayerful reply—and then tossing them a Sunday school teacher's lesson book or, in this case, a camcorder or editing system, and saying, "Thanks, you start in two weeks."

Whatever happened to the idea of training and equipping these servants and giving them the tools they need for fulfilling—successfully and effectively—the ministry they're being asked to do? The same applies to using video in youth work. There are several realistic ways for anyone interested in working with video (or any other "new" media in ministry) to come up to speed. Seminars, conventions, community colleges, books, videotapes, audio tapes, local video production companies, local experts, Web sites, Internet support groups, forums, and libraries—there, you have a dozen. A starting point. Call 'em, then equip 'em.

11. What accessories or peripherals will be needed?

Once again, your answer to question 1 (*What do you want to do with video?*) will determine what on a long list of gizmos, gadgets, and other accessories you'll need to complement your primary video equipment. Think tripods, headphones, cables, filters, monitors, stands, microphones, lights, cases, batteries, furniture, and Snicker's bars. In fact, this question is a good one to ask someone already doing what you *want* to be doing with video.

12. Who needs to be involved in the process?

From the very start, get the people on board who need to be on board—key student leaders, key congregational leaders, committees and subcommittees, et cetera. Your answer to this question will no doubt be different at different stages of building the vision, acquiring the gear, and actually using video in your ministry. The familiar principle of people supporting what they "own" applies here. Involving the right people and people groups is vital to your success, as every youth worker knows if they've been doing youth ministry longer than 27 minutes. Ignore this question at your own risk.

By the way, these 12 questions make an effective template for outlining your written proposal to the church council for establishing your youth ministry video budget.

Five ways to acquire equipment

Let's stop asking questions and start getting gear. There are five ways to get your hands on video production equipment. (Well, there *is* a sixth way, but it's illegal in all 50 states and breaks an item on God's Top Ten list. So we'll let that one go.)

Donations

The method of choice in all things youth ministry. Don't underestimate the potential of simply asking for video equipment from schools, colleges, businesses (especially video production businesses and TV/cable stations), and even families in your church itching to upgrade to new video technology. A lot of used video gear sits in storage rooms, closets, and basements all over this country. The Internet is a terrific way to get the word out about your divine digital desires—just be very specific in communicating what you want. Avoid the temptation to sketch a general plea for unspecified free equipment.

People respond much more willingly to specific needs and ideas. Help them understand the important part they'll play in impacting young lives and your ministry with youths. Find a creative way to thank them (a videogram produced with the gear they donated?) and recognize their contribution publicly. Hey, you're a youth worker, after all—you know this drill.

Ask, receive, record. A very nice three-step process.

Renting

Renting or leasing gear is probably not a viable option for most youth workers, but it may fit some. The upside—you don't have any large, initial purchasing costs. The downside—depending on how much you pay annually to rent video gear, that money could have been put toward your own equipment.

Chances are you'll use the renting option for special events requiring some video equipment you may not own yourself—perhaps a portable large screen for that outdoor drive-in theater outreach. Or possibly the multicamera/video switcher/five-headset communication system for your annual Christmas production. Buying gear you don't use regularly doesn't make financial sense.

Whether or not you have your own camera to record a special event, you may want to rent time on an editing system,

Ways to Get in Gear

BUYING USED

BUYING NEW

RENTING

BORROWING

DONATIONS

which allows you to take advantage of powerful production tools without having to buy them. Again, the odds are good that a local videography company is willing to heavily discount hourly or daily editing-suite rates for a ministry such as yours. (Jay has built relationships with dozens of high school and college students, as well as with youth workers who rented editing time—with or without him as operator—to put together a video program for their youth ministry.)

Finally, renting may be a persuasive way to demonstrate to the congregation—especially the powers that be—the potential for creating your own video programs. When they see the wonderfully creative job you did on your video and hear the response of the students and parents, it could go a long way to getting the ball rolling to purchase some of your own gear.

Just this week Jay rented a professional SVHS linear editing system he no longer uses to a Christian camp—a college student there has the vision for producing weekly highlight tapes for the campers throughout the summer camping season. Great guy. Great idea. Great ministry.

Buying used

This is a legitimate—and possibly the most practical—option for youth ministries of any size to start growing in video-enhanced youth ministry. With just a little research into the gear you're looking for, and the person or company you're buying from, some wise used video equipment purchases can be made. Just a few months ago, Jay in Pennsylvania sold his used miniDV camera to a film student in California via the internet (Jay upgraded to another miniDV cam). That same month, he found a whole bunch of used video gear on the internet from a video guy in Detroit.

Sources for used equipment include trade magazine classifieds, video production companies of all sizes and in all locations, and the Internet. There are a large number of classified-ad forums just for video production equipment, both consumer and professional. When it comes to used video technology, it's a buyer's market every day, since every day newer technology is arriving. Last year's latest and greatest are very nicely priced for the electronically aware shopper.

Here are some details to look for and ask about when buying used video gear.

• How much wear and tear has the equipment seen? Used gear from schools and colleges tend to be pretty beat up from the several hundred hours of use by hundreds of different users.

• How was the equipment maintained? Was it serviced regularly? Was it serviced *ever*? What is its repair history? Just think of the questions you would ask if you were buying a used vehicle.

• Why are they selling?

• What did it cost them annually to maintain, service, and repair the gear?

• Can they demonstrate to you that the unit performs as you expect it to?

• Are they willing to give you a three-day or one-week return period with a full refund if you're not satisfied?

Buying new

For those who can, consider these tips for buying new, off-the-shelf video gear.

• Buy from reputable dealers who stand behind their sales with a no-questions-asked return policy of 30 days or more.

• Keep all receipts in a place where you can find them when you need them.

• Keep all packaging. You'll need it if you have to send the unit in for repair.

• Buy extra batteries (for camcorders) or bulbs (for video projectors). The one rechargeable battery that came with your camera is inadequate for most of your portable videotaping needs. Two *additional* batteries are even better.

• Buy the best you can afford. (We'll say it again. *Buy the best you can afford.*)

• Shop around once you've decided on a particular model. Put free enterprise to work for you. All things material are negotiable.

Borrowing
This week's video happenings

Wednesday, Amanda Ferkins: "My parents have a video camera they said we could take on this weekend's canoe trip."

Saturday, James Lyle, standing on the bow of Amanda's canoe: "You guys want to see the biggest splash ever made with a canoe oar?"

Monday, you: "Dear Mr. & Mrs. Ferkins, I am writing with a heavy heart to inform you that your Canon XL-3764U digital camcorder does not float..."

Borrowing is risky. Jay has a road kill, pancaked Panasonic camcorder to prove it. It's a great prop in youth skits requiring a demolished video camera. (A student keeps bugging Jay to let him borrow it and take it on a flight, at the end of which he wants to open the overhead storage compartment and tearfully demand of the flight attendant, "What have you done to my new video camera?")

No matter how you obtain the video technology necessary for reaching your goals and purposes for youth ministry, don't get discouraged if equipment doesn't accumulate as fast as you'd like. Be patient. Put every piece of gear to use immediately and imaginatively. You may be pleasantly surprised how one good contact, one connection, leads to another—and before you know it, you're set up with just the right video system for your needs.

6

Editing
Cookin' Up All That Raw Footage

"I love birthday cake. I just don't like the raw ingredients."
—Jonas Delariso

No one in his or her right mind would bring to a dinner table of friends a roast on a fine platter—uncooked. Nor would they bring the ingredients of, say, French bread, unmixed and unbaked—some yeast in this bowl, raw flour in that one.

Yet that's exactly what folks do every day—serve up unprepared, unappetizing, *unedited* video to polite but nauseated audiences of all ages. Hence the motto of this chapter, and possibly the most single most important principle in this modest book:

Unedited video was never meant to be shown.
It was meant to be edited, *then* shown.

Raw footage is, well, *raw*. Unprepared. Uncooked. Unservable. Unwatchable. Editing is what cooks up the ingredients. Even at the most basic levels, editing is what makes video watchable. Think of every TV, film, video, homegrown, Hollywood-made production you've seen—or any other visual program you've enjoyed. What made the difference? Probably the fact that it was edited—and hopefully edited well.

So you don't think you have time to cook the video dinner before serving it? The utilities needed to cook a dinner make it too costly for you? Convinced you can't learn high video culinary art?

First, you're probably wrong on all counts. While camcorders have been around for some time and are common among the general public, video-editing packages have generally been out of public reach—until the last three or four years. The availability of fine editing tools for the general public has exploded recently with a proliferation of low-cost, high-powered, easy-to-use, computer-based editing packages.

Second, think for a moment of the two kinds of videos your students have spent their short lives watching:
• Edited video, without themselves in it (TV, movies, video productions rented or bought, and the like).
• Unedited video, with them in it (Uncle Charlie, mom and dad, friends, the youth group's summer trip, et cetera).

Isn't it time you gave them what they deserve, what most students never see...

edited video starring them
(either on camera or as producer/director)

Granted, the normal, unedited, shoot-and-show video that the typical youth group is accustomed to seeing itself in is okay. Fine. Kind of effective. But when you see kids' reaction, involvement, and impact of themselves in an *edited* video— why then you'll know it's in a league all its own. This is the kind of homegrown video they show their friends, write about in their e-mails and diaries, and talk about over school lunches and at the mall on weekends. They're what they write you thank-you notes for. And think about more than they'll ever tell you.

From this day forth, it's our hope and dream that you see your camcorder as an ingredient gatherer—a digital shopping cart in which you pile all the great raw material for cooking up just the right video for the right youth ministry application.

Editing is where the power is

And the creativity. And a menu full of intriguing, audience-pleasing possibilities.

In simplest terms, editing is *selective duplication plus spice.* It's choosing which video clips to copy, then rearranging and shortening them. (Ah, yes, shortening—a chief function in editing. More about that later in the chapter.)

The spice of editing consists of the enhancements you add to your productions, giving your video that extra zing—enhancements such as music, sound effects, titles, special effects, and narration, to name just a few. All this selective duplicating and adding spice can be done traditionally (tape-to-tape) for tradiional types or digitally (computer-based) for you postmoderns. Both are viable choices, each with advantages and shortcomings.

Two ways to edit video

We'll try to be objective about this, but it's hard. Nudge us if our bias shows. First let's get an quick overview of both kinds of editing, then—if you care—a more detailed look at them, with pros and cons, advantages and shortcomings.

There's tape-to-tape (or linear) editing, and then there's computer-based (or digital) editing. (We're not counting in-camera editing, although we suppose that would be a third kind.)

Linear editing is building a master tape from beginning to end, in a straight line, just as the word *linear* implies—from one tape, the raw footage, to another tape (what will become your production master). Linear editing is creating the scenes in the order they'll be seen.

Computer-based, or digital editing, on the other hand, means you can edit any scene in any order. You can build your master from the inside out, from the end to the beginning—you can leapfrog wherever you want, editing here, editing there, rearranging edited scenes, splicing scenes, adding clips you forgot about—and when you're nearly finished, you create the opening scene. Nothing has to be done sequentially. With digital editing, many changes can be made at any time, most of them heart attack-free. And therein lies its overwhelming power and pleasure: Random acts of editing are not only possible, but expected.

Tape-to-tape (or linear) editing

Until relatively recently, editing video (and film) was done in a sequential, or linear, fashion:

1. By placing the unedited camera footage into one machine, the editor could shuttle back and forth until he found the desired scene. At this point he paused the playback deck (usually the VCR).
2. Then our traditional editor would shuttle the recording deck (usually the editing deck) to the "in" point, which is where the selected scene from the playback deck is to be dropped in (hence, the "in" point).
3. The recording deck is then placed in the record/pause mode, and the edit is performed by the editor simultaneously pushing play on the playback deck while "unpausing" the record deck—thus copying that scene onto the production master.

Sounds a little cumbersome when put into words. Hey, we could have made a video and showed you instead! The most basic means of accomplishing this tape-to-tape editing is the two-finger approach (and no, this does not make the method "digital"!): Using both hands, one to control the playback function on one deck and the other to control the record function on the other deck.

The more common method—and it's incredibly more accurate and less frustration-producing—is using some kind of edit controller, a piece of gear used in linear (tape-based) editing to control the player and the recorder. An edit controller greatly facilitates the editing process, giving you control of functions in both decks from one panel. If you find yourself in a linear-editing situation for whatever reason, do everything possible to obtain playback and recording decks with an editing con-roller. The typical consumer VCR in most homes does not have this feature.

Here's a short list of some good and bad aspects of linear editing.

First the good news:

There's plenty of used linear-editing gear available (when this book went to press, at least), since the arrival of digital editing technology is replacing linear editing equipment.

With linear editing, there's no need to enter your footage into a computer. You can piece your program together immediately.

Linear editing is easy to learn. Linear editing is straightforward, and with a little practice, just about anyone can be off and running, accomplishing basic editing tasks.

That's about it for the good news. Now for the not-so-good news.

Linear editing takes a long time. The time factor can quickly overwhelm the easy start-up capabilities of linear editing, except in the most basic of video projects.

Changes are difficult to make in linear editing. Very little flexibility is available in linear editing. If you finish editing your production master and then decide that the 30 seconds of Susie doing Jamie's hair is just a little too long, you're stuck with all 30 seconds of primping—because trimming down that scene will be a major headache with linear editing. If you *really* need to shorten that scene, you have three options (and you won't like two of them):

. Go back to that scene, edit it (that is, shorten it), and then reedit every scene *following* that one. (Yuck!)

2. Copy your edited production master to another tape, but pause the recording deck to shorten the haircutting scene, then continue to record the remainder of the production master. Like a Publisher's Clearinghouse envelope in your mailbox, this sounds good at first—but it's not. Generation loss kicks in

Editspeak

Assemble edit. Recording both video and audio in sequence immediately following previous material. Consecutive edits would then form a complete program.

CG. Character generation—that is, titles or computer-generated text. Also included in the broader term "graphics."

Cut. Making a transition from one scene to another instantly. The cut is the most common transition/edit on the planet. ("Cut!" is also what the director screams when you mess up your lines. Also what happens to your youth ministr budget on an annual basis.)

Dissolve. A type of transition/effect from one video clip to another where Image A fades out as Image B fades in, with the images overlapping and mixing through the transition. The second most common transition/edit on the planet.

Dropout. Not the high school variety. Still, a bad thing. A "drop-out" is a tiny portion of videotape surface that loses its recorded picture information; this mar shows up as thin horizontal streaks or lines. The poorer the quality of your video tape, the more dropouts it will contain. The same goes for formats—the higher the quality (like miniDV), the fewer the dropouts.

Edit controller. A piece of gear used in linear (tape-based) editing to control the play and record functions. This greatly facilitates the editing process and gives you control of functions in both decks from one panel.

EDL. Edit Decision List, a list of time code "in" and "out" points for a particul production or segment in a production. Not very visually exciting, but helpful.

Flying erase head. A feature on the recording head of VCRs and camcorders that provides seamless, glitch-free edits.

Frame. 1/30 of a second. Each second of video contains 30 frames. Even though you can't see the individual frames as you can with film, they're still ther

big time when you start making copies of copies, which is how this solution works. The resulting picture quality is lousy. The lower the quality of the original format/footage, the lower the quality of each succeeding generation will be.

3. There is a livable and likeable solution provided you have

Generation loss. No, this doesn't refer to your students being inferior to you. It refers to the loss of picture quality when you copy one video to another. The copy is one generation below its source in quality. The raw footage right from the camera is first generation. Copy that, and you've got a second-generation tape. You can take it from here.

Insert edit. A video insert edit replaces a portion of the video with other footage, but without changing the audio. An audio insert edit replaces the sound of a clip with a different audio, but without changing the video.

Jog/shuttle. Not an astronaut's exercise—it's another term used in linear editing. Some VCRs (usually those designed for editing) have a jog/shuttle dial that allows for fast tape handling, both forward and backward. This feature also allows for accurate positioning of either the playback or record deck in setting up edit in and out points.

Snow. It's white stuff, but it's not cool—at least not in your videos. Snow is what you see on your TV screen when playing a blank videotape. Not pretty. An electronic eyesore. Many VCRs and projectors are designed to show a blue screen (as opposed to snow) when they sense there's no recorded signal. Keep snow where God intended—outside on your lawn, not in your video productions.

Storyboard. A series of cartoon-like sketches illustrating key visual sequences (shots, scenes) of a video production. Also includes notes and info about the audio track. Storyboards are used extensively in preproduction to help everyone know what shots are needed.

Time code. A system for referencing and synchronizing any frame of videotape. A time code is like a clock recorded onto your tape, including hours, minutes, seconds, and frames. A typical time code number looks like this: 01:34:23:22 (that is, 1 hour, 34 minutes, 23 seconds, and 22 frames into the video).

one simple feature: audio/video insert, also called audio/video dub. With this feature you can insert another clip over part of the haircutting scene without creating a nasty glitch at the "in" or "out" point. If you have a camera or VCR with this feature, you can shorten the marathon hair scene and still be home in time for supper.

Linear editing involves too much generation loss.
Your right-out-of-the-camera footage is first generation. The copy you make while editing (production master) is second generation. Make copies of *that* for students and parents, and now we're talking third generation.

This three-generation process is a common one for producing videotapes in linear fashion. The first-generation footage looks rather good on many cameras and in most formats. The second generation is usually not too bad either, especially if you start with SHVS, Hi8, or miniDV. The third generation starts showing serious signs of generation loss, and the more you work with video, the more quickly you'll start noticing these signs: loss of clarity, colors bleeding through their edges, an overall deterioration in sharpness, a general muddiness in the footage—these all point to the inherent weakness of tape-based editing called generation loss.

Digital (computer-based) editing...or "Look Ma! No tape!"

The list of reasons for choosing the digital editing route is growing in leaps and bounds. Although the good far outweighs the bad, in the spirit of full disclosure we'll identify potential downsides to the digital-editing revolution taking place.

First, the bad news. Don't worry; it ain't that bad.

Some people have computer phobia. They've decided they can't learn to use anything computer-based. Fortunately, the exact opposite is true of virtually all teenagers today. You're most likely to run into this malady among your older volunteers.

Endless upgrades. Although it's relatively inexpensive to get started in digital editing, the addiction to having the latest, greatest, fastest, and coolest upgrade or accessory can push up your costs a lot. If, however, you avoid this temptation and make the most of what you have for another six months before upgrading, you can stretch your production dollars a little further.

Now for the good news—and it's really good!

Digital editing is tremendously flexible. As mentioned earlier, changes are almost encouraged in the nonlinear world of digital editing. That much-too-long haircutting scene in the aforementioned example would have taken about 11 seconds to trim on a computer-based editing system, and that's on a slow day.

Digital editing technology is constantly improving. In all things electronic today, it's faster, cheaper, smaller, and more powerful than yesterday. A video hard drive costing $3,000 several years ago now goes for a couple hundred dollars. CPUs (computer processing units) seem to improve every several weeks. What took tens of thousands of dollars to do in video only a decade ago can now be accomplished for a couple thousand dollars or less.

Digital editing is easy to learn and getting easier. Software developers have finally gotten the message that no matter how powerful their programs are, if they aren't easy to use—and we mean *really* easy—then people just won't bother. It's no understatement to say that with some digital editing systems, someone with zero computer or video experience can learn how to perform basic video editing procedures in 15 to 30 minutes. Of course, like anything else, mastery requires persistent practice and study. But the learning curve on many of today's video editing programs becomes less of a curve every year.

Kids know computers, the main tool in digital editing.
No big revelation here. A simple, yet powerful fact. Just about
all teenagers know how to use computers or learn quickly how
to use them.

Basic editing tips and techniques

The purpose of editing is to take unwatchable, unenjoyable,
ineffective raw video footage and transform it into a watchable,
enjoyable, and effective video program. Editing gives you and
your students the power to—
   • tell a story
   • correct and delete mistakes
   • condense or expand time
   Whether you're using the most basic of the basic approaches
to editing or the latest and greatest digital editing suite, your
video programs will benefit from these suggestions. And no
matter who ends up editing your video productions—students
much of the time, we hope—these ideas will spur your creativity and remind you how to take advantage of the power of the
editing process.
   Some of you may find just enough info here to make you
thirsty for more, while others would drown if you tried swimming through all these tips. So just skim the list until you see
something interesting, something that connects with you and
your level of expertise.
   In any case, once you and your students get a taste of the
unlimited potential, impact, and expressions possible through
video editing, it's our humble opinion that you'll wonder how
you ever lived *before* editing your videos!

Fit the pacing to the production

If you're putting together a collection of nature scenes to a wor
shipful song, or any song with a slow-to-moderate tempo, you
probably don't want to edit your scenes one after another at a
pace of one second per image or clip. The speed or pacing of
the images would be too fast for the music and the overall
impact you want to have on the viewers.

On the other hand, a sports-highlight video should move along at a much faster pace, with music that does the same. This whole idea of pacing is best learned through actually editing, and also by observing other productions.

Black Beauty

Always, always, always begin every production you ever edit with a minimum of 10 to 15 seconds of solid black before the first image or sound. For your edited master, 20 to 30 seconds is appropriate. Why? Because when it comes time to make copies from your master, the recording VCR takes several seconds to actually start recording after you push the record button.

Do the same thing at the end of your program. After the credits roll and the music stops, continue recording for at least 30 seconds to avoid the snowstorm that will arrive on your screen when the VCR hits the blank section of tape. Another reason to start all programs with some black is because the beginning segment of videotape is the portion most exposed to dust, heat, moisture, and other video-killing elements.

Use flying erase heads

This is a strange term but a vital feature on the recording VCR/camera if you're using a tape-to-tape (linear) editing approach. When you pause the VCR with flying erase heads while recording/editing, and then unpause it to add the next scene, the edit you created at the pause will play back smoothly and seamlessly without disrupting or breaking up the video images around that edit. Flying erase heads are found on all VCRs designed for editing, though not on typical household VCRs.

Maintain continuity

A fancy phrase that simply means to maintain a sense of direction. In a chase scene, keep the subject moving the same direction. Don't have a subject moving right to left in one shot, but in the next shot moving left to right. It confuses viewers, and it's tacky (unless, of course, you're using it for comedic effect).

Match the action
Similar to the continuity rule. If one scene shows an actor approaching a door from the outside, and the next shot is from inside, make sure you capture the actor opening the door—in other words, try to match the action so it doesn't look like a time warp or like the actor "jumped" from one place to another in an unrealistic amount of time. Matching the action won't be an issue in many of your informal, fun, or highlight-type productions.

Edit on the action
Just watch TV or a movie for 30 seconds, and you'll see this editing principle all the time. Take the above walking-through-the-door example: A good place to make the switch from the outside shot to the inside shot is at some point *in the action* of opening and entering the door—not *before or after* opening and closing the door. Same with fight scenes—edit *on* the punch, not before or after. (Hey! What are you doing with fight scenes in your youth ministry videos, anyway?!)

Shoot for the edit
Anytime you record video while anticipating ways you can use that footage, you are shooting for the edit.

Last year while on a mission trip to Mexico, Jay recorded the entire song his youth group sang in front of their new Mexican friends' church. Not because he wanted to show the entire group singing the entire song on the video, but because he was anticipating using *just the singing*—that is, the audio—as a perfect soundtrack for much of their Mexico highlight video.

Or imagine this: Your student video production team is putting together a three-minute, person-on-the-street segment on your upcoming hot topic. While the kids are videotaping the interviews, they also get shots of the interviewer listening, passers-by watching, funky street scenes, and so on. Shoot more than you need. Remember, you're gathering ingredients for cooking up a great video. All these shots give you flexibility in editing and allow you to cover a multitude of video sins.

K.I.S.S. (Keep Inserting Short Scenes)

Last month Jay coached a youth pastor friend of his through editing a winter-retreat highlight video. The youth pastor later told Jay that the video was a great hit, but some of the scenes he included would have been much more effective if he had cut them in half.

Now he knows, and you do, too. Violate this suggestion, and you can KISS effective video goodbye. Kids, by the way, know this rule instinctively. When we edit with students, or when they do the editing, this is rarely a problem.

Organize your footage

Label all your videotapes immediately after you remove them from the camera. Depending on the type of video you are creating, you may want to catalog your footage on paper or computer so you know what and where every shot is without having to play the tape. This is an indispensable step when working with linear editing equipment since that system requires you to shuttle back and forth to find the next scene in your production.

Keep special effects special

Just because your editing equipment can do 298 different spins, twirls, warps, wipes, strobes, mosaics, slides, and bounces doesn't mean you have to use them all in the same production. Follow these two basic rules: 1. Use special effects purposefully; 2. Less is often more.

Avoid jump cuts

When you edit from one shot to another very similar or matching shot (both close-up, both wide, and so on). If you create an edit between two similarly framed scenes or between two scenes with similar focal range or background, there will be a "jump" at that edit point that's uncomfortable to the viewer when you play back those two scenes together.

To avoid jump cuts, simply zoom in or out or change angles before shooting the next scene. It will keep you from recording yourself into a corner.

When you must shoot 'n' show

Sometimes, rarely, unfortunately, there will be times when—for whatever reason—you'll videotape knowing that the tape you pull out of the camera is what will be shown. (Do not pass Go, do not collect $200 worth of editing). This is called in-camera editing—shootin' and showin'. It's risky, but with a pinch of forethought, it can still be somewhat effective. Just make it the rare exception.

Keep your scenes short, shorter, and shortest.

Unless there's a lot of action, a lot of people, or a lot of interest for some other reason, keep your scene length from three to seven seconds long. This will obviously vary, but remember, what seems normal and interesting when you're taping will transform itself into an eternity when viewed with a group.

Be still and know that people are listening.

This is a nice way to say "be slow to speak" (James 1:19, if you must know). You will be severely tempted to add your own remarks as you videotape. Resist this temptation with every fiber of your being. Unless your last name is Seinfeld or Carrey, you'll probably suffer intense embarrassment when those off-the-cuff statements come blasting over the sound system. And they will blast, since your mouth was only about six inches from yonder built-in camera microphone at the moment of utterance.

Don't fade to and from black repeatedly.

The safest thing is not to do it at all except for the beginning and ending of the tape. The fade on most cameras takes several seconds, which tends to slow down your production immensely if you do it repeatedly. Fading to and from black indicates the passage of time or changing location.

Avoid in-camera special effects.
Unless you have a specific effect for a specific purpose for a very short amount of time, avoid using the camera's digital effects. If you do use any, make sure you know exactly how to use them, and set them up before you start recording.

No date/time stamp.
Never. Ever. None. At all. Forever. Eternally. Stop it.

Play live music while showing the video.
If you're showing inner-tubing highlights on your winter retreat or snow camp that you just shot that afternoon, play some music while watching the clips on the big screen. The music mixed with the natural sound of the tubers simulates exactly what you would have done in editing—mixing music and natural sound. Much youth ministry raw footage lends itself to this approach.

Use the camera's in-camera playback/review features.
Some cameras have a feature that allows you to rewind the tape for several seconds or more and then automatically return to the record/pause mode. This could be your only salvation for eliminating those totally unwatchable scenes moments after they are captured. A good feature to take advantage of, but you must act quickly before recording additional scenes—or else the offending scene will come back to haunt you publicly.

Know your camera's tape-handling abilities and style.
Most cameras vary slightly from model to model regarding how they handle tape when entering the record/pause mode from standby or from being completely powered down. Know by practice and by experimenting with nonessential projects

how long it actually takes for your camera to start recording once you hit the record button. Discover how much it back-threads or "backspaces" when you go from its playback/VCR mode into its recording/camera mode. As a not-so-ancient, not-so-Chinese proverb notes, "Know thy camcorder." Without the pleasure and power of editing, if you ignore this tip, you might be unpleasantly surprised by what you see or don't see come showtime.

Don't eject and insert the tape between scenes or shooting times.

Each camera varies in its ability to thread and unthread video-tape accurately when loaded and unloaded from the camera. If the camera you're using creates a glitch (a nasty breakup in the playback image) whenever you load and unload the videotape, then avoid doing this at all costs. Another reason not to rein-sert the tape is that there's a good chance you'll lose the last several seconds of the previous scene because the camera "backspaced" while threading the videotape through the recording heads. Keep the tape in the camera until it's full.

Tell your subjects the tape will be shown unedited.

Best done before you push the record button. This is the gold-en rule of videotaping. Embarrassing your on-camera talent is not the goal, and if you record their interview or antics and then say, "Oh, by the way, we're showing this tape unedited tonight to the entire youth group," you're a good candidate for authoring a book entitled *How to Lose Friends and Negatively Influence People Using Video in Youth Ministry*. Sell 'em. Shoot 'em. Show 'em.

7

Showtime!
Putting Your Best Footage Forward

So you shot your own homegrown video, then followed the
rules of basic-but-effective editing—
• You trimmed the digital fat.
• The sound effects you synchronized with the action are guar-
  anteed to bring the house down.
• Some clever and well-designed, non-red-colored titles start
  and end the program.
• A handful of impressive, tasteful video special f/x are sprinkled throughout.
• And the music? There won't be a dry eye in the house after
  the closing three-minute montage of images set to the latest
  tearjerker tune (lyrics about God, lasting memories, lifetime
  friendships, missing you, and so on and so on).

Now it's your job to make sure your audience (whether 12,
120, or 1,200) sees the video at its best. What a waste it would
be for you, your kids, and your youth leaders to have poured
their hearts into this masterpiece only to have it crash and
burn come showtime because someone forgot to make sure

the projector was set up and working correctly.

This urgency assumes that the video production is a quality one—or at least as quality as you had time, money, and equipment to make it. An ideal, state-of-the-art presentation will not make a poor production look good. A video's power and effect lies in both production and presentation—yet poor presentation will compromise a good video.

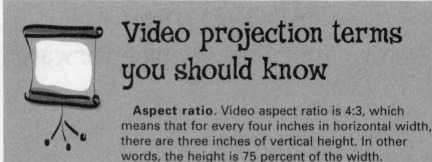

Video projection terms you should know

Aspect ratio. Video aspect ratio is 4:3, which means that for every four inches in horizontal width, there are three inches of vertical height. In other words, the height is 75 percent of the width. Implication: projected video/computer images will not fill a square screen. Square screens are not good for video projection.

Ceiling projection. A setting found on many projectors, which optimizes the image when projecting from a ceiling-mount projector installation.

DLP. Digital Light Processor, another type of new technology used in video projectors. (Also, Jay's surname without the vowel.)

Fixed-focal-length lens. A type of video projection lens without zoom capabilities.

Freeze. A nice feature found on some projectors that allows you to freeze any projected image. This, of course, then allows you to interrupt your presentation source (PowerPoint, VCR, live camera) without disrupting the projected image.

Keystoning. A distracting effect on a projected image when the video projector is positioned below the screen. The effect consists of the image's top edge being wider than the bottom edge. Many video projectors offer anti-keystoning capabilities to compensate for less-than-optimum projector-to-screen setups.

Intro to video projectors

Video projectors have become significant tools in youth ministry—and for good reasons. These slick inventions finally made it possible to show any video program on the big screen (as opposed to a TV), for large or small audiences. In fact, you don't even need a screen. The whitewashed broadside of a barn door (well, a *big* barn door) would work pretty well—as

LCD. Liquid Crystal Display, one type of technology used in video projectors.

Lumens. The term measuring a projector's image brightness. The higher the lumens rating, the brighter the projected image.

Magnify/reduce. A projector feature that allows you to zoom in and out on portions of the projected image.

Minijack. The type of audio input found on most projectors. A cable connects it to your computer's audio output.

Reverse image. A feature found on most projectors that allows you to reverse the projected image for either front or rear projection.

RGB input/output. The 15-pin connection used to hook a computer directly to the video projector.

Video projector resolution. By matching a computer's maximum resolution with a projector's maximum resolution, you can take full advantage of the optimum picture quality of both. The following are in order of increasing resolution—
 • **VGA**. Video Graphic Array; indicates a digital image resolution of 640 x 480.
 • **SVGA**. Super Video Graphic Array; indicates a digital image resolution of 800 x 600.
 • **XGA**. Indicates a digital image resolution of 1,024 x 728.
 • **SXGA**. Indicates a digital image resolution of 1,280 x 1,024.
 • **UXGA**. Indicates a digital image resolution of 1,600 x 1,200.

would any other white surfaces, such as houses, walls, church buildings, tractor trailers, sailboat sails, bedsheets, tent ceilings, and beached albino whales.

All of today's video projectors connect directly to a VCR or computer and display the video image in sizes ranging from four to 40 feet and higher, depending on the power and brightness of the video projector. The brightness of video projectors is measured in lumens. The higher a video projector's lumens rating, the brighter the image.

Like everything else electronic, the units are getting smaller, lighter, cheaper, and brighter. Ultralight video projectors can weigh less than three pounds.

How to buy a video projector

Shop around
The video projector market is very competitive, so check out at least a few dealers of new and used equipment. Once you decide on a specific model, compare and save.

Test-drive it
If at all possible, especially when buying new, ask for a rep to bring a couple of projectors from the dealer to your typical venue—your youth room or sanctuary, say—and demo the units for you under realistic conditions. Set the lighting conditions as close to what they will be like when you show videos. Jay did this when his church bought its first projector. The rep brought two units to the church at 9:30 on a weekday morning so Jay could duplicate the average lighting conditions during his church's normal Sunday morning worship service. Such careful test-driving eliminates all doubts about a projector's ability to meet your needs.

Know what features you want and need
The list of features, like your list of reasons for being in youth ministry, grows each year. If you want to wirelessly control

your computer mouse with the video projector's remote control, make sure the unit you buy has this feature. (Many projectors have a remote sensor for this built right into the side of
the unit.) If you'll be using a specific brand of notebook computer with the projector, then hook up that computer and make
sure the projector displays its screen clearly and with the reso-
ution you need.

Talk to an owner

You should be able to find someone, either locally or on the
internet, who owns the exact model you're considering. Ask
her why she bought it, why she would or wouldn't buy it
again, what she likes and doesn't like about it, what she paid
for it, where she got it, and so on.

Make sure there's some kind of return policy

Video projectors can be a big-ticket item (anything over $49.99
is big-ticket for most churches), so protect yourself. If you
aren't tickled pink with your purchase, don't buy it unless you
can return it within 30 days, no questions asked. Longer is better. An extended warranty is also wise, as long as the extra
cost is reasonable.

Buy an extra bulb

Yes, replacement bulbs for video projectors can run into the
several-hundred-dollar range—but you'll need some sooner or
later, so get 'em before you're at North Woods Wilderness
Retreat Center and a bulb goes out in the first five minutes of
your six-hour, projector-dependent seminar 50 miles from the
nearest gas station and five hours from any store that carries
projector bulbs.

More and more congregations are buying and using video projectors every year. Although the initial expense seems steep (to the finance committee, not to you), video projectors can be used in many ways and many places—except for those permanent ceiling-mounted units, which are tedious to unbolt and take with you on retreats. After a couple of shows, even the finance committee members will see the deal they got.

So hit the lights, push play, and pass the popcorn.

The 10 Showtime Commandments

Let's assume you're using a video projector to show a student-created production at your youth group's Christmas party or banquet. Break any of these commandments, and you might as well just wear a sign on your back all night that reads, "Go ahead and make fun of me!"

THE FIRST COMMANDMENT

Thou shalt arrive early, set up, and test all equipment
A tremendously small price to pay, but vital to the success of your premiere. When you discover at 4:30 p.m. that the VCR is broken or missing, you at least have an option or two. Come show time, however, your options for replacing a VCR are zip.

THE SECOND COMMANDMENT

Thou shalt have a backup copy
You were a good youth worker and obeyed The First Commandment. Then the curse of Job struck during your test, and the VCR ate your only videotape. Your *only* production master. Hence, the precaution of making *two* copies of your production master.

THE THIRD COMMANDMENT

Thou shalt position the screen for all to see
Test the viewing angles from the extreme seats—the ones on

the wings, in the back, and in the very front. If you find viewing problems from such angles, allow people to reposition themselves just for the video presentation.

THE FOURTH COMMANDMENT

Thou shalt remove objects from the projector's path

Jay's church uses not a screen, but the wall behind the pulpit, since it's large, flat, and white. The only problem is the large floral arrangement on a shelf along the bottom edge of the wall. So unless someone remembers to remove the flowers, the lower quarter of every video scene features flowers.

The other usual suspects include microphones, music stands, pulpits, lecterns, banquet table settings, candles, balloons, light fixtures, musical instruments, wall vents (tough to move), stage props, and the six-foot-ten guy in front of the projector beam who, of course, doesn't have any idea it's *his* head casting the shadow over a third of the projected image.

THE FIFTH COMMANDMENT

Thou shalt have quality sound

Much of your program's effectiveness will result from a well-produced and well-presented soundtrack. Let's assume you've got a great soundtrack with well-recorded music, narration, and sound effects. Now that you've got good sound on your video, why play it through Barbie dollhouse-quality speakers? A lot of video projectors have built-in speakers—which unfortunately deliver small, thin, tinny, and powerless sound.

For groups of 50 or more, you'll almost always want to use a separate sound system when projecting and presenting your videotape production. Of course, if you are showing it in a room or auditorium with its own sound system, by all means use that system. Run your sound from the VCR directly into a channel of the soundboard rather than to the video projector. (By the way, this is one of those crucial items to test, as per The First Commandment!)

THE SIXTH COMMANDMENT
Thou shalt have a big enough screen

If the Third Commandment is about avoiding a big-enough screen in a bad position, this commandment is about avoiding a too-small screen in a good position. There are several rules o thumb for matching group size to screen/image size.

• Screen width should equal but not exceed half the distance from the screen to the first row of seats.

• Screen width should equal or exceed the distance from the screen to the last row of seats, divided by six.

• If the above two calculations give you significantly different results, use the larger of the two screen widths.

• Screen height should equal or exceed the distance from the screen to the last row of seats, divided by eight.

THE SEVENTH COMMANDMENT
Thou shalt not use a square screen

Video is not a square format. It has a 4:3 ratio, meaning that fo every four inches in horizontal width, there are three inches of vertical height. Square screens are not made for video, so don' try to fill up a square screen to the edges in an attempt to make it look like a big TV. You'll have to shrink your projected image to fit in the upper parts of the screen until the left, top, and right images are aligned with the edge of the screen, leaving the bottom a blank and barren wasteland. Or you can enlarge your projected image to fill the square screen, which means a large portion of your scenes will spill out over the sides of your screen. Not pretty.

The remedy? Use a 4:3 video screen. Very attractive, no visua distraction.

THE EIGHTH COMMANDMENT
Thou shalt use the best screen surface possible

This commandment is not as critical as it was a half century ago because projectors have become brighter and brighter. Still, screen surface is important. With the exception of textured, barn-like surfaces chosen for their atmospheric effect, the goal for projection purposes is to use a screen surface that highlights your projected images, be they video images or computer-generated graphics.

Here are acceptable choices, according to this commandment.

• Simple matte white—an all-purpose surface that reflects light almost equally in all directions and appears consistent from even the widest viewing angles.

• In long, narrow venues, a glass-beaded surface may be your best bet.

THE NINTH COMMANDMENT
Thou shalt love darkness rather than light
Even with the brightest video projectors, you must control ambient light that spills or leaks into the room. Close those curtains, dim or turn off the lights, and by all means kill any light source that shines directly onto the screen.

THE TENTH COMMANDMENT
Thou shalt applaud thy students' efforts—loudly and standing
All youth workers know the incredible need that youths, as well as the rest of us, have for affirmation and encouragement. Involving them in video production presents umpteen opportunities for encouragement—the greatest opportunity of which could be the "World Premiere" of a student-produced video. After the audience sees their names in the credits, get them out of their seats amid the inevitable applause following homegrown youth ministry video productions. Have bogus, semi-bogus, and legitimate awards to present to the crew immediately after the credits roll.

Unlike the Ten Commandments, you can improve these by customizing them for your youths and youth ministry. Be lavish, not slavish.

Front or rear projection?

You can project an image on the front of the screen (the side the audience is sitting on) or—provided your screen is translucent—from behind the screen.

The advantage of **front projection** is that you can place the screen directly against a wall, requiring little if any space between the screen and the wall. This keeps the screen from protruding into the room space, providing the best possible viewing angles from the sides (depending, of course, on the layout of the room). Front projection also gives a remote control's infrared signal easy, line-of-sight access to the projector.

Rear projection has a few things going for it, too. First—and, some believe, foremost—is the removal of the video projector from the audience area to "out back," where it's out of the way and protected from sprinting five-year-olds, an ample supply of which most churches have been endowed with. Furthermore rear projection makes it a lot easier to enclose the area surrounding the projected beam and protect it from ambient light. In effect, you could create a tunnel-like enclosure—a veritable room—through which the rear-projected image passes in total darkness. This is not possible with front projection.

The primary disadvantage of rear projection is the space needed behind the screen—from 15 to 40 feet, depending on the size of the screen and the focal range of the projector. If you want to use rear projection, make absolutely certain your projector and screen size will work in your venue so there's no installation-day surprises. Finally, your remote control signal, presumably out front with you, may have difficulty reaching a rear projector. Curtains, partitions, and similar obstructions tend to block reception, although signal boosters are available that can overcome this problem, depending on the degree of obstruction.

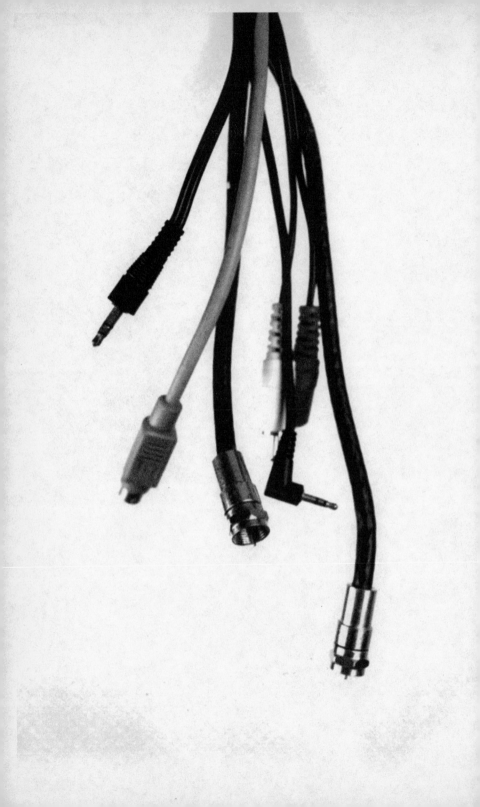

8

Getting Connected
Born to Be Wired

Good communication is as important for electronic components as it is for humans. If you understand your signal path—that is, the path your signal takes from one piece of gear to another—and what types of connections must be made each step of the way, you can speed your electronic travelers on their way without damaging the rather fragile image they carry to their final destination.

Four video interconnectivity principles

INs are connected to OUTs

Every video camera, video projector, VCR, and video-equipped computer has audio/video in and out connectors. The ins are for bringing signals into that unit. The outs are for sending sig-

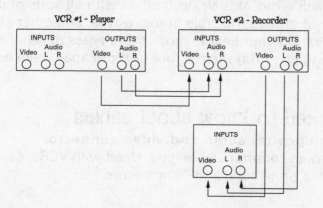

nals *from* that unit. For example, if you want to copy a video from a VCR to a VCR, your signal path would look like the diagram on page 95.

All cables are not created equal
Humans are, audio and video cables are not. Use the best cables you can find or afford. How sad it is for your pristine out-of-the-camera images to suffer permanent damage en route to their editing destination because you wanted to save $2.95 on a bargain cable. Your image quality is limited to the weakest link in your video chain. Make sure the cable is not that link.

The longer the journey, the greater the loss
The further your signal has to travel, the greater the potential for loss—loss of strength, loss of clarity, loss of color, loss of overall stability. (Very much like youth group road trips: The further you travel, the greater the potential for loss: loss of sleep, loss of health, loss of temper, loss of general stability, loss of job.) Keep your cables (and your ministry trips) as short as possible.

Avoid cable conflicts
Cables don't always get along well with each other. For instance, you don't want to run your video and audio cables parallel and adjacent to an electrical power cord. The power cable will beat up on the signals carried by the a/v cables, and the signals will arrive at their destination with all sorts of digital bumps and bruises, horrible hums, waves, and other electronic injuries. Do your best to cross these types of cable at 90-degree angles or run them a foot or more apart from each other.

All you need to know about cables
RCA (or composite) audio and video connector
This is the most common cable type. Used with VCRs, camcorders, video projectors, and TV monitors.

The People Who Brought You this Book...
invite you to discover MORE valuable youth ministry resources.

Youth Specialties has three decades of experience working alongside Christian youth workers of just about every denomination and youth-serving organization. We're here to help you, whether you're brand new to youth ministry or a veteran, whether you're a volunteer or a career youth pastor. Each year we serve over 100,000 youth workers worldwide through our training seminars, conventions, magazines, resource products, and internet Web site (www.YouthSpecialties.com).

For FREE information about ways YS can help your youth ministry, complete and return this card.

Are you: ☐ A paid youth worker   ☐ A volunteer   S=480001

Name_____

Church/Org. _____

Address ☐ Church or ☐ Home _____

City _____State _____Zip _____

Daytime Phone Number (_____) _____

E-Mail _____

Denomination _____ Average Weekly Church Attendance _____

The People Who Brought You this Book...
invite you to discover MORE valuable youth ministry resources.

Youth Specialties has three decades of experience working alongside Christian youth workers of just about every denomination and youth-serving organization. We're here to help you, whether you're brand new to youth ministry or a veteran, whether you're a volunteer or a career youth pastor. Each year we serve over 100,000 youth workers worldwide through our training seminars, conventions, magazines, resource products, and internet Web site (www.YouthSpecialties.com).

For FREE information about ways YS can help your youth ministry, complete and return this card.

Are you: ☐ A paid youth worker   ☐ A volunteer   S=480001

Name_____

Church/Org. _____

Address ☐ Church or ☐ Home _____

City _____State _____Zip _____

Daytime Phone Number (_____) _____

E-Mail _____

Denomination _____ Average Weekly Church Attendance _____

BUSINESS REPLY MAIL
FIRST-CLASS MAIL   PERMIT 268   HOLMES PA

POSTAGE WILL BE PAID BY ADDRESSEE

YOUTH SPECIALTIES
P.O. BOX 668
HOLMES, PA 19043-0668

I..III.I..II....I.I.I.III.I.I..II....II....II.I..II

BUSINESS REPLY MAIL
FIRST-CLASS MAIL   PERMIT 268   HOLMES PA

POSTAGE WILL BE PAID BY ADDRESSEE

YOUTH SPECIALTIES
P.O. BOX 668
HOLMES, PA 19043-0668

I..III.I..II....I.I.I.III.I.I..II....II....II.I..II

SVHS (or S-video, or Y/C) video-only connector

S connectors offer noticeably higher picture quality than RCA/composites. S-video connections are found on SVHS and digital gear (miniDV, Digital8, DVCPro, DVCam, and so on).

FireWire (or IEEE1394, or i.Link)

Here's the highest quality of the three connections. FireWire allows you to transfer audio and video via the same connection with no generation loss. This digital connection is found on all Digital8 and miniDV equipment and on all computer-based editing solutions designed for editing videotape shot on digital video cameras. Because of its higher data-transfer rates, FireWire is becoming the connection of choice for nonvideo peripherals, such as scanners, external hard drives, and so on.

The four most common video hook-ups (or *configurations*, for you sophisticated types)

The following hookup guides help you with the most common connections and setups you're likely to encounter in youth ministry video situations. When we refer to video connections, always use the highest-quality connection your equipment allows. For instance, if you're using an SVHS camera or VCR for playing a videotape and a video projector or TV equipped with SVHS-type inputs, then use SVHS cables instead of inferior RCA/composite type connectors.

These setups are just a start. The idea here is to learn the basic approaches for hooking up your video gear and understand how the audio and video signal paths flow. Think of the path logically (the video starts here and has to go out to here and in to there...), and use the cables and connections to take that signal along its journey from one component to another. Most equipment owner's manuals can help with a variety of common equipment setups to accomplish all kinds of video tasks.

Playing a videotape from a VCR/camcorder to projector/TV

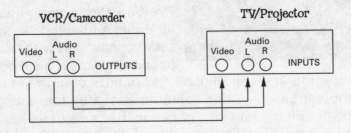

1. Connect the video "out" of your playback unit (VCR/camcorder) to the video "in" of the TV/projector.

2. Connect the audio "out" of your playback unit to the audio "in" of the projector/TV. It's often better to run the audio into a separate sound system or mixing console, which offers much better sound quality and power than the much smaller and less powerful speakers built into most TVs and video projectors.

3. Select the audio/video input mode for your projector/TV corresponding to the audio/video inputs used. If S-video connectors are available on both units, use them instead of the RCA video "in" and video "out" connectors for superior picture quality when playing videotapes recorded in SVHS or a digital format such as Digital8, DVD, or miniDV.

Tape-to-tape editing setup: beginner's level
You could use two VCRs or a VCR and a camera for the following setup. To keep this as simple and clear as possible, we'll

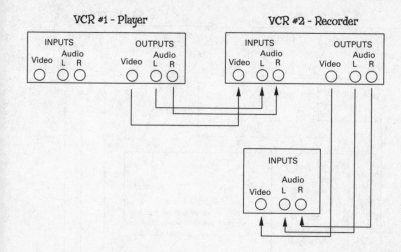

assume you're using two VCRs. If you're using a camcorder for either the playback or record unit, or both, then just substitute it in the diagram above. The connections are the same.

Always hook up a TV/monitor to your recording unit so you can see exactly what you are or aren't getting on the tape you are recording onto.

1. Connect the video "out" of your playback unit (source) to the video "in" of your record unit (destination).

2. Connect the audio "out(s)" of your playback unit to the audio "in(s)" of your record unit.

3. Connect the audio "out(s)" and video "out(s)" of the record unit to the audio/video inputs of a TV.

4. On the record unit, use the input select features (either a button or an on-screen selection) matching the input being used.

5. On the TV use the input select features to match the input being used.

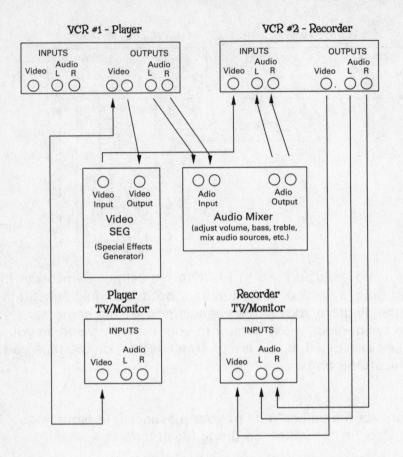

Tape-to-tape editing setup: intermediate level

In this setup let's assume you've added an audio mixer, a second TV/monitor, and a video mixer/SEG (special effects generator) to give you more power and flexibility when editing your video productions.

This setup is a nice step forward in video production, giving you many more editing options and production possibilities without costing a lot. The level beyond this in tape-to-tape editing would be the use of an edit controller—see "Editspeak," page 70—which would give you even greater editing accuracy and speed.

1. Connect the video "out" of your playback unit (source) to the video "in" of your SEG unit.

2. Connect the video "out" of your SEG to the video "in" of your record unit.

3. Connect the audio "out(s)" of your playback unit to the audio "in(s)" of your audio mixer.

4. Connect the master audio "out" of your audio mixer to the audio "in(s)" of your recording unit.

5. Connect the audio "out(s)" and video "out" of the record unit to the audio/video inputs of a TV.

6. On the record unit use the input select features (either a button or an on-screen selection) matching the input being used.

7. On the TV use the input select features to match the input being used.

Basic computer-based (nonlinear) editing setup

This setup outlines the hookups going to and from your computer-editing system. The biggest variable in this editing equation is obviously the computer-editing system itself. That will determine the amount of power, speed, and flexibility available to you—plus the number and type of audio/video inputs and outputs available. You can add components on the way to and from the computer, so to speak, to enhance your production possibilities (like digital video effects units, video switchers, audio mixers, CD players, et cetera). The more powerful (and thus capable) your nonlinear editing system is, the less need you'll have to add them to your editing system.

1. Connect the video "out" of your playback unit (source) to the video "in" on your computer video card.

2. Connect the audio "out(s)" of your playback unit to the audio "in(s)" on your computer audio card.

3. Connect the audio "out" and video "out" of your computer audio/video card to the audio/video inputs of a VCR or camcorder.

4. On the record unit, use the input select features (either a button or an on-screen selection) matching the input being used.

5. Connect the audio "out" and video "out" on the recording unit (VCR, camcorder) to the audio "in(s)" and video "in" on your TV/monitor.

6. On the TV use the input select features to matching the input being used.

9

Goin' Live to the Big Screen

Some of your favorite and most effective applications of video in youth ministry won't involve recording, editing, and playing back videotape at all—you'll be going live.

Here's the basic equipment you'll need to use live video in youth ministry.

- A video camera
- A display device (a TV or a video projector and screen/wall/flat white surface of some sort)
- A cable (connecting the camera to the display device)

Technically, that's all you need to get started—but you can beef up this bare-bones minimum in a hurry if you want. The same principles we discussed in chapter 8 apply here. The same camera tips and techniques listed in chapter 10 apply to using the camera live.

One of the most common applications of live video in youth ministry is recording conferences, worship services, and concerts where you see the projected image of people on the stage or platform enlarged on big screens positioned next to the stage area. Another term for this is *Imag* (EYE-mag), short for image magnification. Perhaps your own congregation is already using live video for your worship services, youth events, or concerts.

Let's look at some of the benefits of going live at these kinds of events.

Going live gives the audience a better view of people and objects on stage.
Since two of the keys to powerful communication are eye contact and facial expression, why not give that experience to everyone in the house via large-screen Imag? Now, even from the cheap seats, everyone can see the gleam in that speaker's eye, the sweat rolling down the drummer's forehead, the tear trickling down the actor's cheek. Go to any large conference, and Imag is standard fare—because convention planners know that Imag makes every seat in the house a good one.

Going live generates a higher level of excitement and engagement.
Having Imag in place at your events and in your services simply gives the entire audience a greater sense of being a part of something big and powerful. Impact and involvement are increased dramatically, which is exactly what your speakers, musicians, singers, drama teams, and worship leaders want.

Going live involves more teenagers in the video ministry.
Someone has to operate those cameras, computers, and video switchers—and more often than not, your have teenagers who would love to be a part of the video team and part of the service or event. No matter how simple or sophisticated, Imag capabilities open the door to involvement for more of your students.

Finally, see the Ideas section of this book on page 124 for live video ideas.

10

Improving Your Servo
(*Servomechanism, That Is*)

56 Tips for Better Video in Youth Ministry

Here ya go! Nearly five dozen video-shooting principles and rules that are especially helpful in youth ministry video production—principles that will benefit you and your video productions while still allowing plenty of room for creativity. There's no sequence here, just a quiver full of shooting tips, techniques, and plain ol' good ideas for bringing home a trophy every time you get an itchy trigger finger. (Or trigger thumb, as the case may be with most camcorders.)

56 tips and tricks of the trade for better video

1. Put a tape in the camcorder.
Silly. You knew that.

2. You aren't ready until it's steady.
Postmodern, shaky footage aside, your goal should be to avoid the shakes at all costs. For shooting stationary or pseudo-stationary objects, get a tripod. If the camera is a-shakin', the footage ain't worth takin'.

3. Focus, focus, focus.
Unless you're shooting a drama on the gradual healing of the blind man in Mark 8 ("I see men as trees walking"), let's try to keep everything nice and sharp, 'kay? Manual focus is more reliable than autofocus in many situations. If you're unsure, 30 seconds of experimentation should tell the story.

4. Don't shoot into a light source.
Sure, there'll be times when it's just not possible for you or the subject to move, but in most cases, the human behind the camera doesn't realize that a silhouetted image in the viewfinder means they're shooting into a light source. The usual suspects include the sun, windows, and artificial lights of all varieties.

5. Get close-ups!
Far and Away makes for a great Hollywood title, but as a videotaping motto it means dull footage, especially when it comes to people and animals. Look at most youth group photographs and some typical home-video footage, and you'll see immediately how rare and wonderful a good close-up is. How close is close-up? If the distance from their waists to their heads fit in the frame, you're not close enough.

6. Don't use in-camera special f/x.
Yeah, we know we told you about the cool effects available with the current crop of video cameras when we defined digital effects earlier in this book, but go easy with 'em if you use them at all. Special f/x that show up in every scene of footage quickly ceases to be special. They're a kind of digital Calvinism—once they're recorded, they can't be lost. Ever. Besides, most of these f/x can be added in editing where and when it's appropriate.

7. Disable the date/time stamp.
If we had a nickel for every time someone brought video footage to us with the question, "Can you remove that distracting date and time stamp recorded on the bottom of this two-hour tape?" we could buy Paramount Pictures by now.

"Sure we can remove it," we're screaming on the inside. "Let's take this Exacto knife and cut it out!"

Instead we smile blandly and say, "No, but we can cover it up in editing with a very unsubtle black square."
If you see it in your viewfinder, you will see it on your tape. (In most cases.)

8. Use an external microphone.

An external microphone is simply external to the camera—a handheld or lapel mike—as opposed to the internal microphone built into the camera. This advice applies particularly to those instances when you're videotaping interviews and other on-camera speakers—any noise and voices all around you compete with the interview subject's voice, and usually drown it out.

9. No extended recording speeds.

This is becoming less of an issue with the new digital formats since they hold their picture quality much better when using extended recording speeds—that is, LP (Long Play) instead of SP (Standard Play). This is a non-issue with 8mm and Hi8 since they don't have extended recording speeds on their cameras. But with VHS, VHSC, SVHSC, and SVHS formats, avoid the temptation to save money and videotape by extending your recording times with the extended recording speed option. Use SP only. Save EP for recording that six-hour TV miniseries on your home VCR.

10. No audio decapitation.

Audio decapitation occurs when you're videotaping someone speaking (person-on-the-street interviews, et cetera) and you tell her, "Go ahead" at the same instant you push the record button on your camcorder. They instantly start talking, but the camcorder doesn't instantly start recording. Which means that when you take your interviews home to be edited, they all start with the interviewee's second, third, or fourth word. You guillotine the "head" of their statement each time you started and stopped recording. Simple solution: push record, wait three seconds, then cue your actors.

11. Change angles.

Mixing up your shooting angles makes your productions much more interesting. Experiment with extreme angles (high, low,

slanted, et cetera). Here's a simple sequence to follow:
1. Shoot.
2. Stop.
3. Move.
4. Shoot some more.
5. Stop.
6. Move.
7. Shoot some more.
8. Repeat sequence.

12. Shed some light on the subject.

Good light is the key to good video. Most inside-the-house lighting is woefully inadequate. So simply turn on some more room lights or use a portable camera-mounted light. It makes a world of difference.

13. Watch TV differently.

Watch TV and movies with an eye for what's happening with angles, close-ups, lighting, audio, and editing techniques—and soon you'll have all kinds of ideas you can apply to your homegrown productions. (It's probably better to keep your visual education to yourself, though. When icy Winslet releases icier DiCaprio into the deep after the *Titanic* sinks, the last thing your date or spouse needs to hear is, "What a great angle!")

14. Just once, watch your raw footage with your youth group.

This is a one-time learning experience, for a videographer's ego seldom survives this lesson a second time. What felt normal and authentic while shooting becomes glaringly obnoxious, repulsive, and embarrassing when you see your own unedited "techniques" displayed in front of a group. You'll laugh out loud with the kids to hide your excruciating discomfort, but meanwhile you be dying inside because of how much you were swinging the camera left to right, commenting out loud every few seconds within inches of the internal microphone, keeping the camera at your eye, holding the record button while eating lunch in order to get some "realistic footage," zooming in and out without ceasing, and weren't holding any shot steady for more than two seconds if at all. The two of us learned lessons this way. It was painful.

15. Honor the rule of thirds.

Divide the screen or viewfinder into thirds with two horizontal and two vertical imaginary lines—like tic-tac-toe, or the opening screen for *The Brady Bunch* (with Alice in the middle, remember?)—and use them to help you frame your subjects better. Here's the rule: Rarely do you want anything dead center. Dead center in video scene framing usually kills interest and quality. Instead, position your subject at one of the intersections of these imaginary lines—that is, at a point a third or two-thirds away from the edge of the frame.

Taping a youth group newscast, for example? Frame the anchor so that her eyes are a third of the way down from the top of the screen. Don't center her eyes.

16. Edit your videos before showing them.

Like we said before, unedited video is meant to be edited, not shown. Every video program you'll ever purchase is an edited program. Every movie you'll ever watch in a theater or on a VCR or DVD player is edited. With the cost of editing gear—and especially computer-based editing equipment—within the reach of nearly every budget, there's no excuse for subjecting any audience to the tribulation of viewing unedited video. Yes, there are always some exceptions (even in this book's third section of video ideas), but use this rule 95 percent of the time. Please, for the sake of your audiences!

17. Tell a story.

Use your camera—better yet, use your editing—to condense everything you want to say into a short story. If you're videotaping your youth group ski trip, don't simply videotape the kids on the slopes skiing (a challenge in itself). Instead, capture short clips as kids load the vans and leave the church. Record interesting sights en route—the sign entering the ski area, the kids putting on their skis, the slopes, the kids coming off the mountain, everyone back at the lodge, kids signing your fresh cast, and finally the trip home.

18. Use filters to produce special visual effects.

As with still photography, a multitude of camcorder filters are available for creating unique visual effects—colored filters and neutral-density or polarization filters, to name two. Most well-equipped video dealers carry them. *Experimentation* is the operative word.

19. Use a clear filter to protect your lens.
When you buy your camcorder, also get yourself a clear filter to permanently screw onto the front of the camera lens. The clear filter won't affect your video images or camera functions, but it *will* protect the lens from cracks, scratches, and other expensive mishaps that would otherwise result in the expensive replacement of the lens. When you're caught in the crossfire of a frosty assault of incoming student-launched snowballs and suffer a direct, frontal hit, you'll be glad you armored your lens earlier with the filter.

20. Lead your subject in the frame.
A quarterback leads his receiver when passing to him—he throws the ball ahead of where the receiver is at the moment of release. In video, "leading" means creating more space in front of your subject than behind him. The rule applies anytime you videotape someone doing anything not directly facing the center of the lens.

If you're videotaping Josh running to first base, and you're next to that baseline, position him on the far left of the viewfinder so there's space ahead of him to run "toward." When he rounds second and heads for third and is now running from your right to your left, reposition him to the right side of your viewfinder. When he's tagged out at home and lets slip a spontaneous, vivid expletive, you shut the camcorder off and pretend he's in the *other* youth group.

21. Always carry extra batteries and tape.
Much of your video shooting in youth ministry will be the portable, battery-powered variety. Once you've missed an important shot—like when Nicole finally ascended the platform and was halfway to her diploma and the outstretched hand of the principal when your camera flashed the ominous E for empty, then shut down—you'll probably remember to charge and pack extra batteries before you hit the road.

22. Shorten the length of your scenes.
A full minute panning over those unique but inanimate turtle eggs you discovered seemed like a good idea at the time. But

when played back for your group, it becomes nothing less than painful to sit through. If there's one thing MTV has taught us about video, it's to keep things moving. If you had bothered to edit the turtle-egg video, you would've noticed and fixed the over-run. When in doubt, shorten the scene—then shorten it some more.

23. Label all videotapes.

The fast road to severe electronic suffering is leaving unmarked videotapes containing irreplaceable footage lying around. Experience isn't the best teacher, but it *is* the most painful. Not to mention the frustration of trying to find a program or scene you just know is in that pile of tapes...*somewhere*.

Minimal info to write on all videocassettes: event name, date, and length of footage. Better yet: a three-ring binder or computer database of catalogued video footage, with simple, brief descriptions of each scene on the tape.

24. Store your videotapes vertically.

Videotapes have a longer shelf life when stored standing on one of their narrow edges instead of lying flat. When standing upright, the tension of the videotape on the reels is better maintained, preventing the sagging that decreases the life span of the videotaped signal.

25. No "zoom abuse."

Next time you watch a movie or TV program, take mental note of how often the director zooms in or out on a shot. The answer is, not often. Agree with yourself to follow suit. Use the zoom between shots to set up different perspectives or "frames," but there's usually no need for viewers to go along for the zooming ride.

26. Use the manual zoom...sometimes.

Some cameras have the option of switching off the motorized zoom, allowing you to zoom manually. You won't be able to zoom as smoothly as the motorized zoom, but you can create some dramatic effects—like the crash zoom, a very fast manual zoom in or zoom out, best suited for sports and action scenes. Just practice a couple times on your subject before hitting that red record button. And use it sparingly. As with your budget, a little bit can go a long way.

27. Don't leave too much headroom (or too little).

Another framing tip: Don't leave too much space above the top of your subject's head. It creates an uncomfortable and unbalanced composition, as if your subject is sinking into the bottom of the screen. Too little headroom, on the other hand, and you're getting into decapitation.

28. Start your scenes with an establishing (wide) shot.

When you show the "big picture" first, it gives the viewer a sense of context for what follows. Very common on TV—first the entire building is shown, the next scene cuts to a room that we logically assume is *inside* the building (although in reality it was in a studio maybe half a continent away from the building, but that's a subject for another exposé). Like the rule of interpreting Scripture by establishing the context, your viewers will be able to interpret your scenes if you establish the context right up front.

29. Use headphones when using external microphones.

If only you'd checked your sound with headphones while you interviewed your entire youth group individually, you wouldn't be stuck with three hours of the finest footage for the program *Today's Teens Tell the Total Truth: A Lip-Reader's Odyssey*. Rather than the silence of the lambs, you would've preferred some audio—so wear headphones to make sure you're getting it.

30. Protect your investment from its natural enemies.

Some things just don't mix—like video gear and sand, water, humidity, extreme cold, or dust. If you must shoot on a beach, wrap your camera in a small towel or invest in a water/sand resistant housing especially designed for your camera. Without such protection, even if you think you've kept the camera away from the surface sand, be assured there *is* sand blowin' in the wind that will find its way into the innards of your video gear. One barely visible particle of dirt or sand on those finely crafted spinning video heads, and suddenly you're holding the fanciest paperweight in town.

31. Use an external monitor.

Especially when you're recording a long program from a stationary position with electricity nearby. By connecting your camera to a small television monitor via the camera's video-out connectors, you can save yourself the eye and neck strain that's commonly acquired from constantly peering into the small eyepiece of your viewfinder. Plus you can gain a more accurate perspective of your footage.

32. Preplan your larger productions.

You probably don't need to do much preproduction planning for shooting video at your Super Sunday Summer Splash. But when it's time to produce that original video production of a modern Good Samaritan, you won't regret investing in some quality preparation for each step of the program. Props, costumes, permissions for location shooting, script writing, shooting times and dates, transportation—these are but a few of the action items on your director's to-do list.

33. Use sound effects.

It's amazing the difference sound effects can make in just about any video production, especially for humorous programs. You can either simulate the required sounds or take them from any number of sound f/x CDs or Web sites that offer free sounds for your downloading pleasure.

34. Always be on "red" alert.

Video is a color medium, of course, and the present systems don't like red, a color that tends to bleed, or move outside the lines of whatever's red, especially in the nondigital formats. Avoid red even in creating titles for your videos. Highly saturated or neon reds are the worst. In situations where you don't have control over on-screen colors, don't worry about it.

35. Watch for tiny patterns in clothing.

Instruct your onscreen talent to avoid wearing clothing with small checks, herringbones, and narrow stripes. These patterns strain video's ability to reproduce them accurately and create a very distracting effect.

36. Use photographs in your videos.

Transferring photographs to video can be a tremendous source of production material for all kinds of youth ministry productions. You can get your photos on video several different ways, but the easiest is to use your camera on a tripod or copy stand. A copy stand is a platform with a vertical post designed to mount a video camera so it aims directly down onto the platform, thus providing easy capture of photographs, printed graphics, and even small objects. The image can be recorded to tape and then edited, or the camera signal can be fed directly into a computer editing system and saved onto the computer's hard drive without ever being recorded to videotape.

37. Learn the exposure limits of your camera.

If your camera has the option of overriding the automatic-exposure functions, experiment with manual aperture and exposure under a variety of light conditions, both natural and artificial. Surfaces lit too brightly can "burn out" and surfaces that are too dark turn grainy, lifeless, and lose their color quickly.

38. Use an audio mixer.

When recording any event or program in your church's auditorium or sanctuary, take advantage of the (hopefully) available soundboard/mixing console—feed your camcorder from one of the soundboard's master outputs.

When editing or shooting anywhere else, however, your videos will benefit immensely by improving your audio signals with an audio mixer dedicated to your video system. Audio mixers come in all shapes and sizes, including one just right for your video-production needs. Check out your local music or a/v store, or browse through the stores' catalogs.

39. Use simple props.

So what if Elisha's chariot is a customized wheelchair? That's half the fun and effectiveness of your production. The human imagination is much more effective and inexpensive than going for letter-perfect prop replicas.

40. Clean your lens.
Check it often, and clean it often. Get some camera lens cleaning fluid and cleaning paper, available at any camera shop.

41. Use a shoulder strap.
We're talking safety and convenience here. Let's keep "On the way I dropped it" in the playground tunes, not in your *Diary of a Depressed Youth Worker* memoirs.

42. Practice first, tape second.
Who said you could hit the record button without first practicing your shot? Granted, this advice isn't suitable for all things unrepeatable, like weddings, but if you're videotaping in a setting that affords you time to set up your shot, then practice your move, your zoom, your combination of both—then go back and tape it for posterity. Vital when shootin' and showin'—when there's no chance for editing.

43. Create your own homemade special f/x.
It doesn't matter how you get the f/x you want, because all that counts is how it looks on the screen. So check out the myriad of poor-man solutions for creating quasi-high-end special effects such as smoke, fire, titles, "accidents," and natural disasters. In fact, the cheesier the better when it comes to youth ministry video.

44. Use high-quality cables.
Don't scrimp on cables—they're the pipelines by which your components talk to each other and transport your fragile video signal to your completed production.

45. Minimize generation loss.
Avoid making a copy of a copy of a copy of—you get the idea. Unless you're using a digital connection (FireWire) to make duplicates, your creative masterpiece will suffer greatly with each generation.

46. Add smooth moves to your production.
Every car, pickup truck, wheelchair, golf cart—to name just a few—are potential camera movers, with which you can give

your productions that professional and creative touch lacking in videos that are all "stand and shoot."

47. Capture that emotion.
Video is an emotional medium, so don't overlook its power to communicate strong emotions to viewers. That means close-ups of people. Match the medium with the message and the emotion.

48. Take advantage of macro.
The macro feature allows you to tape an object within millimeters of the lens. A world of possibilities and unusual images awaits those willing to experiment a little.

49. Know thy camera (I tape, therefore I am).
Take an hour some Saturday afternoon and simply fool around with every button, setting, and feature of your camera—because this is about the only way you'll learn how it works before you're in the moment (and then the moment is gone). Same goes for your editing system, sound mixer, VCR, and microwave oven.

50. Be teachable.
Everyone has some good ideas for making video productions better. But it's only the teachable few who ever truly "hear" these ideas. Students and adults alike have much to offer each video production. Don't go it alone.

51. Use audio-editing software.
Today's computer-based audio programs are powerful and affordable. Manipulating the sound on your video can enhance its impact, humor, and most other results you're after, too.

52. Super-size it!
Why debut your long-awaited production on a 27-inch TV when you can borrow a video projector, turn out the lights, and display it on the big screen? The impact soars exponentially, not to mention the atmosphere and audience involvement. (And don't forget to match the big picture with big sound!)

53. Go back to school.

Go ahead, sign up for that night class or attend that seminar on some aspect of improving your videography abilities. Buy that book or other resource designed to help you make the most of your gear and your built-in talents.

54. Follow the leader.

Don't record your completed program at the absolute beginning of the videotape. Always provide a leader—at least 10 seconds of recorded black before any sound or picture. This makes duplication much easier, because recording VCRs need several seconds to go from stop to record. Plus the first 10 to 15 seconds of videotape is the most easily damaged since it's more exposed to light, dust, and air.

55. Cut out the jump cuts.

A jump cut is an edit with little or no change in the camera position or framing. The subject appears to instantly jump from one position to another as if in some hyper time warp. Not a pleasant sight. Simply change angles or reframe your subject between shots (or fix it in editing).

56. Have fun.

But then, you suspected this one all along. Good—you're on the right track!

VIDEO IDEAS GALORE!

A Plethora of
Projects & Possibilites

Video Ideas for Teaching

Define-a-Word
A compelling way to direct kids' attention to the subject you're teaching. Before your teaching day, record kids in your group (or on campus—or *any* kids, at the mall, and so on) to define a key word in your lesson.

Back to the Past
Interview your church's seniors for any old reason—a practice that builds cross-generational bridges, preserves the legacy of seniors' lives, gleans wisdom from the wisest of the wise, encourages a typically overlooked segment of your congregation, and teaches teenagers to value people much older than themselves.

Roller Coaster Ride
Play back this clip whenever you want to talk about the ups and downs of any process—family relationships at home, romance, the Christian life itself. The next time your group goes to a theme park, take along the camcorder and record the roller coaster ride as best as you can. Just be sure to first turn on EIS (Electronic Image Stabilization). Not only do you get incredible video coverage, but also the screams and yells are priceless.

Word Association
Basically like Person-on-the-Street Survey (page 144), but not silly—instead, an introduction to your lesson. If your lesson is about the book of Genesis, for example, ask random passersby questions like, "What do you think of when I say *Abraham*?...What does creationism mean to you?...What were the plagues on ancient Egypt?" Don't editorialize their responses, which—correct or incorrect—make a compelling springboard for your lesson.

Did Someone Say *Training*?
If you're in a position to equip *everybody* doing *anything* in ministry, video is the perfect way to give them the training they need—not to mention how reusable the training is in video form (provided the content doesn't become obsolete

oon). Monthly or quarterly, put together a 10- to 15-minute
video for your adult leadership team. Include an upbeat sum-
mary of what the youth ministry is doing (thanks to the volunteers' work), some encouragement, announcements for
upcoming events, and a snippet of training on one aspect of
youth ministry. Make enough copies for all your volunteers.

The Lighter Side of Small Groups

A humorous way to provide serious teaching and training.
Decide whether you're making this video for adult facilitators
of small groups or for your students. Then list the small-group
dos and don'ts you want to cover (for a wonderful list, check
out Youth Specialties' *Help! I'm a Small-Group Leader!* by
Laurie Polich). Then lead your student actors and one adult
actor in a rehearsal before you record: In the 10- to 20-minute
video, they should demonstrate how *not* to conduct a small-
group meeting or study. One student talks too much, another
too little, the leader is ill prepared, and so on. Here are some
variations on "the lighter side."

The Lighter Side of Teaching

A parody video of all the things *not* to do while teaching the
Bible to teenagers. Show it to your volunteer leaders and
Sunday school teachers. For example, actors demonstrate
"Five Things to Never Do While Teaching." Never insult a student (a teacher blasts a student for not knowing her Bible),
interpret the Bible carefully (the teacher explains that Jesus
went up to the mountain to pray because he hated being
around the disciples so much), stuff like that.

The Lighter Side of Road Trips

How not to prepare and conduct a bus or van trip with
teenagers.

The Lighter Side of Song Leading

Actors demonstrate the no-nos of singing too loudly into the
mic, not knowing the words to the songs they lead, or singing
harmony when a group is still unfamiliar with a song.

Video Ideas for Promotion

Pre-Event Announcements

Trying to get the announcements across, but no one is listening? Videography to the rescue! Project your youth group or congregational announcements before the official opening of an event, like the preview ads in theaters. If you make it a loop, the announcements will repeat until the event begins.

New Year's Eve Party

A lot of youth organizations throw New Year's Eve parties to keep kids from problems associated with that last night of the year. Take your camera along and videotape the night. Show the video to the kids in a week or two. The students who attended the party will love it, and the ones who didn't will wish they had. Then use it later in the year to promote the next New Year's Eve Party.

Parent Meeting/Parent Appreciations

During your next parents meeting, show a video of a particular parent who's been especially helpful to the youth ministry. Add a testimonial or two from students whose lives this adult has particularly influenced.

Video Thanks

Record a string of students' thank yous and grateful remarks when someone has been especially generous in any way toward your group—then give the tape to that someone, but not before first showing it publicly.

Highlights and Lowlights

If you tape every youth ministry event, you'll have plenty of fodder for a three- to five-minute highlight tape at your next gathering, raw material for a two- to three-minute promo for the same event next year, short clips for your youth group Web site, ammunition for your killer end-of-year highlight tape, and more.

From Diapers to Diploma

This is a classic parents-will-love-you-forever idea. It's simply a video compilation of growing-up pictures of each graduate. The video can be set to music, sprinkled with special effects, high-lighted with titles, and served up at a grad party or banquet. Great gift. Great encourager. Do it every year.

Reach Out and Tape Someone

Building bridges to the unchurched in your community is one of the highest and best uses of video technology. Taping youth subcultures (skaters, surfers, cruisers, street hockey players, et cetera) and working with them to produce their own highlight tapes has almost limitless potential for relationship building and impact. Just as with pictures, put kids on tape, and they'll do anything (and go almost anywhere) to see themselves!

Video Newsletters

For the digitally addicted. If you can produce acceptable video programs on a regular basis, a video will be the most anticipat-ed piece of mail someone could receive. Youth pastors can use video newsletters to communicate to parents, to the youth min-istry staff, to students—the youth group can use video newslet-ters to stay in touch with high school graduates in college, in ministry, and in the neighborhood. It requires some work, but if you've built a good student-led multimedia team, this could end up being invaluable as well as not just another task you have to do.

Video Brochures

There's no better take-home gift for friends and visitors than a four- to six-minute (no longer than 10) video about your youth group, church, or any other aspect of your ministry. It doesn't have to be fancy to be effective. Typical but effective formats run like this: Begin by introducing yourself as the lead youth worker. Show a brief clip of each program or ministry. Add short testimonials—one from an adult and one from a teenager. Then wrap things up with a personal invitation from you. Remember your primary audience—visiting parents or visiting students—and speak to that audience. A video brochure can go a long way toward bringing people back.

Fifth-Quarter Videos
Make your Fifth Quarter party especially memorable by recording the cheerleaders, the band, the fans, a couple of plays, maybe some moms and dads, and as many kids as you can—then playing the tape as the climax of the party.

Camp Promotions
Hopefully the best way to sell this year's camp is to show last year's highlight video. At the end of your summer camp, put together a seven- to 12-minute highlight video for the kids. Then show it again, two months before the next summer's camp. Last year's kids remember the great time and want to go again. The kids who missed camp get to see the great stuff and won't want to miss this year.

Sporting a New Image
Videotape your town's high school athletic games, matches, or meets—football, basketball, track, wrestling, gymnastics, swimming, whatever—then edit a high-energy highlight tape of 10 or 15 minutes. Offer the tape to the coaches, players, and their families as a gift from your ministry. You can almost guarantee it'll be shown at the school's sports banquet if the video is completed by then.

Go Thou and Do Likewise
As you and your students get more savvy with videography, and as your video ministry grows, and if you live and work in small town—then you and your student team just may be a video resource to the community. Offer your taping and editing services to schools, teachers (offer to tag along and tape their field trips), coaches. Ask libraries and other community groups if they need anyone to teach workshops on any of the various aspects of video. Publicize and conduct your own mini training clinics and seminars for the public, or—if you're in a large church—for other youths, volunteers, staff, and leaders at your church. Invite middle school and high school classes into your "editing room" (okay, so it's only the former equipment nook in your office—it could be a veritable Jerusalem to a ninth grader fascinated by what you're showing him about video editing).

Video Announcement Ideas

Video Announcements with Spliced-In videos

Add scenes from old movies when making the announcements to create curiosity and more punch. If you're announcing your upcoming summer trip, for example, insert a 30-second clip of the space shuttle taking off, with an announcement lead-in saying something like, "Don't be left behind when we launch our incredible summer camp this year…"

Video Announcements with Voice Dubs

Have one student lip-sync the announcements while an off-camera student actually does the voice. The effect is great. Don't let the lip-syncher be too good—it's the slightly unsynched nature of the gag that makes it funny. Give the on-camera male speaker a female voice or mix it up with a 15-year-old and a 45-year-old.

Video Announcements with Strangers

Videotape a group of strangers that your youth group wouldn't recognize to make your announcements.

Video Announcement with Parents

Recruit parents to be the announcement-makers. Kids are always surprised to see their parents on tape.

Video Announcements with Teachers

Get your high school's teachers to make your announce-ments—in their classrooms (or locker room, choir room, wood shop, lab) if possible. Principals, custodians, and bus drivers, too!

Video Announcements with Siblings

When your students are at school, go to their homes and get their younger siblings to announce upcoming events. They're cute and funny, and everyone will tune in.

There are lots more—just ask your students.

Video Ideas for Worship

Natural Worship

First choose a song that helps set a worshipful ambiance among your teenagers. Make a note of the song's length, then go to a peaceful, serene, or otherwise appropriate outdoor setting that you can videotape. Record as many minutes of video as the song is long, and then transfer the song to the video.

Remember to use the camcorder's or VCR's audio in connectors—not the camcorder's mic input—to record (audio dub) directly from the audio source (CD player, cassette deck, and so on).

Baby Worship

Newborns and infants, for some reason, can reflect some distinctive aspects of God's nature. So take your camcorder down to your church nursery and videotape the little tykes playing, observing, and just being wonderful. In editing, add a soundtrack of worship music, and you have a worship-enhancing video.

Elder variation

Record joyful, laughing images of your church's seniors, as well as contemplative and more serious clips, too. Overlay with appropriate worship music. Serve to worshiping group of teenagers or adults.

Live Video Ideas

Not once during these ideas will you push play or record, though you could incorporate video playback or recording of videotape as an add-on for several of them. Showing live video has a lot to offer youth workers who stop for a few minutes and consider the possibilities.

Character Captions

You've probably seen this idea done very effectively. It involves the use of some type of character generator (PowerPoint, MediaShout, et cetera) and equipment that allows you to superimpose text over live video. It's a lot of fun for an audience, especially at large events like concerts and youth rallies.

Here's how it works.
1. Before the show or event, use your titling or text-generating software to prepare some captions—simple phrases or short sentences: *Forgot to put on deodorant this morning, Came here to find a girlfriend, Collects Beanie Babies.* You get the idea.
2. Situate a camcorder, probably toward the front and off to one of the sides, where it can get close-ups of individuals in their seats.
3. While everyone is getting seated and waiting for the show or event to start, your camera operator simply finds good targets in their seats, zooms in so their faces fill the screen, and boom—whoever is controlling your caption software adds the caption superimposed over the soon-to-be-pleasantly-embarrassed targets.

Small Talk

Here's an idea for spicing up your next youth talk, retreat session, or sermon.
1. Mount a video camera on a tripod or copystand (a stand designed to mount a small video camera vertically on a tabletop, available at most video supply stores) so that it points *down* on a table or another flat surface right next to where you're speaking.

2. Make sure the surface is well lit (clamp lights or special lights especially designed for use with video copystands are good).
3. Connect the camera to the video projector...and voilà! You've got a high-tech, twenty first-century show-and-tell device.

Now you can finally use all those object lessons whose objects are super small, even with large, auditorium-sized groups. The smallest object will fill the big screen, though you may need to use the camera's macro feature, which allows you to focus on objects within inches of the lens. There are also macro "lenses" (though they're more like filters) designed for this purpose that you simply screw on the front of your video camera; they usually come in sets of three or four different magnifications. Any photo or 3-D object can be used quickly and effectively in this way.

The Medium Is the Message
Your lesson is about focus, and the importance of keeping it on God. Before your meeting, you set your camcorder on a tripod in front of the room near where you'll speak, then select the camera's autofocus mode. At the appropriate moment in the meeting, you select a volunteer (a plant) to come up and stand 10 or 15 feet in front of the camcorder's lens. This person represents God, you say. (Meanwhile, everyone can see "God" on the big screen.) A bit later in your lesson, select a second volunteer to come up and edge into the picture between the camera and "God"—which will make the automatic focus kick in and refocus on the distraction while "God" is in the background, out of focus, blurry, indistinct. When the distraction moves out of the camera's view, "God" comes into focus once again.

You can take the spiritual applications from there. And to ensure this demonstration's success, you'll definitely want to set up and test it before the meeting, and mark the two positions with tape on the floor if necessary.

Draw Me Nearer
Illustrates how getting closer to something or someone tells you more truth about it. Use the camcorder's zoom feature to demonstrate how the truth of an object or person is unknown, unclear, or misunderstood at a distance—but on closer examination (then you zoom in), more is discovered. Appropriate technique for topics like the character of God, stereotypes, judging others, assumptions.

Random Acts of Projection
So the retreat speaker uses a video projector, huh? Kids are kicking back between sessions, it's raining, they're bored, and someone brings out their little home camcorder and hooks it up to the projector—and let the experimentation begin! This happened at a youth retreat Jay attended once, and it was amazing how some of the students' creative juices got going. Suddenly they were creating special effects using the video camera and screen like the illusion of wall- and ceiling-walking, standing on their heads, or climbing vertical cliffs.

Besides the change of pace it offered the kids, it was a chance for Jay to observe some creative initiative that, 'til then, had been in hiding.

Overflowing Multitudes
Got a crowd too large and a space too small? Set up a video camera or two in the main auditorium, run the camera signals through a video mixer and out the door to an overflow space in the basement or another room, and project the live image to the overflow crowd. Hopefully you already have sound piped internally to the overflow location. If not, you could set up a portable sound system and run sound from the main-event location to the overflow room.

Video Projector Ideas

You don't even need a camcorder for these three ideas—just a video projector and rear projection screen.

Mystery Guest

Next time you have an occasion to bring a mystery guest to your meeting or event for an interview or introduction, sit the guest behind the screen in the video projector's beam so he or she casts a silhouette on the screen. Experiment with different sizes of guest images by having the person move closer to or further from the screen.

Radical Surgery

An old favorite, and it still works. The audience watches silhouettes of a crack (or cracked) surgical team operating on a patient. After opening him up, the team extracts all sorts of unlikely objects from the patient's innards—in silhouette, of course: chains, license plates, stuffed animals, tools, and kitchen appliances. Or convert the surgery into a promotional skit for an upcoming ski retreat. The surgeons pull skis, boots, poles out of the patient. For a work trip, out come tools of all sorts, and for summer camp, luggage and campfire wood. (You get the idea!) Mic the surgeons to catch their comments. You may even want to supply sound effects.

Shadow Plays

Especially effective for elementary-age kids and younger. With rear projection, stage shadow-puppet shows with your hands, stuffed animals, sock puppets, actual Muppet-type puppets, et cetera. Jay had a movie night for seven- to 10-year-olds in his neighborhood, and for 20 minutes or so they shadow-played with the projector beam. Once even a low-key, back-row parent got in on the act.

Video Ideas for Silly Fun

The Stick

This idea was stolen from late-night TV. A professor has created a new miracle gadget called "The Stick" that can do anything. Introduce it this way, then proceed to demonstrate all
the great things "The Stick" can do. It can be a wallet, a kick-
ball, tissue paper, fire hose, dance partner, car, belt—a list of 20
"Stick" demos is just about perfect. At the end, of course, the
professor gives his "And only $9.95 if you order today!" pitch.

Good Morning, America! Breakfast

Arrange with the parents of a student to arrive at the student's
house a half hour before that student gets up for school (be
sure it's a school day!). With two or three other students as co-
conspirators, sneak into the bedroom of the soundly sleeping
student and jostle him awake—getting everything on tape, of
course. Keep the camcorder rolling as you interview the
sleepyhead in various states of consciousness, pick out his
clothes for the day, take him to a local restaurant for breakfast,
and take him to school. If you don't have editing capabilities,
keep the length of the tape to around 10 minutes—only shoot
snippets of each aspect of the morning.

Just the Bedroom

With parents' permission, videotape students' bedrooms while
they're at school. You may want to plant some particularly
bizarre or tame-but-incriminating objects in the room before
you hit the record button. Surprise your group with the playback. Lead your group in rating the bedrooms and award mock
prizes: Most Organized, Messiest, Cutest, Least Navigable,
Least Amount of Wall Showing, and so on.

Group Kidnap

At any time of day, and with the permission of fully informed
parents (who can keep a secret from their teenagers), kidnap a
string of six to eight students, one at a time. Ambush them and
tell them they've got one minute to get ready and leave with you.
Videotape everything, especially the looks on their faces. Then
head for the local food court or pizza joint and hang out and
laugh for a while. (And show the video at your next meeting!)

Prom Date

Follow a couple as they prepare themselves for the prom—or any date, for that matter. You may want two cameras, one following the guy, the other following the girl. Videotape her as she gets her hair and nails done, puts on her makeup, and so on. Get shots of the guy as he gets his hair done, picks up his tux, makes reservations for dinner, et cetera. Interview parents and siblings just prior to "the pick-up." Get just the hot spots of the entire night, not everything. Don't forget to tape a few seconds of interviews with the waiter, faculty chaperon, limo driver, and other crucial folks.

Workplace Interviews

Find out where your students hold down part-time jobs and interview their bosses and coworkers. Ask about their first days on the job or their funniest moments. See if these folks will agree to give false, totally embarrassing answers (scripted by you).

Parent Interviews

Arrange secretly with parents an interview regarding their child (best done while kids are at school). Interview six or eight parents, asking them intriguing and fun questions like whether something outlandish happened the day their sons or daughters were born, how old they were when toilet trained, a memorable childhood birthday, and other similarly intrusive questions. You'll discover parents have some wild stories about their kids. (And the relationship-building potential of a project like this could be huge for you and parents.)

Video Scavenger Hunt

Before kids arrive prepare a list of things they must do while being videotaped in certain locations or with certain people:

- Standing in a public fountain
- Riding the bus, trolley, subway, El, light rail, et cetera, on their knees with their hands over their hearts
- Gathered at, on, around, or beneath a quirky city landmark.
- Standing on the deck of a yacht
- Asking a police officer to show the camcorder two pieces of I.D. that identify him or her
- Reading a picture book to a child (one or two students can do this)

- A male must engage a clerk in a fashionable store (i.e., Saks Fifth Avenue, Macy's, Bloomingdales, Nordstrom) in order to buy a hair accessory for himself.
- With a teacher
- With a waitress at TGI Friday's
- In water
- Hitching a ride
- Picking their noses
- Reading a magazine
- Wearing the camp T-shirt
- In a bathtub
- In a bathtub full of water
- Throwing a pie in someone's face
- Wearing a mask
- Doing jumping jacks
- With the school principal
- Inside a Volkswagen Beetle
- Playing tennis
- Sleeping
- Dancing
- Fake throwing up
- Really throwing up
- Building a human pyramid
- With the senior pastor
- In front of the school mascot
- Having an egg splatted over their heads
- With Madonna
- With a team member's little brother or sister
- In a church praying while sitting on the pews
- Screaming
- Yodeling
- Singing "The Star-Spangled Banner"
- Preaching to a crowd
- In a graveyard
- In a tree

You need about 30 items on the list, and the items should vary in difficulty (100 points for the screaming clip, 500 for the fountain clip). Divide your group into teams. Then distribute your list, including instructions and rules, some of which may include the following.

- Teams must choose only 10 of the items on the list to video-tape them doing.
- Every team member except for the cameraperson must be in the footage (unless indicated otherwise).
- Each video section should be only 30 seconds long (other-wise you'll end up with hours of footage).
- Each team's final video must not exceed five minutes.
- They may combine items—for example, the items "Picking your nose," "Reading a magazine," and "Wearing the camp T-shirt" can be done simultaneously in one video clip.

Once they've done their ten 30-second shots, they head back to the youth room for viewing. View each team's five-minute video, laugh, and judge the winner based on accumulated points.

Voiceovers

Requires simple editing. Record about a half hour of random video clips of students interacting at either a typical or special youth group meeting or event. Later, record your live commentary as a soundtrack over the original audio. When you play the video for the group, your kids will see themselves on the video with your verbalization of their supposed thoughts.

There are two ways to pull off this editing fun.

Method A: Plug your microphone into a small audio mixer and your mixer's audio output into the VCR's audio input. The mixer can convert the microphone's signal to a line signal.

Method B: Use the audio dub feature, which is fairly common on video cameras and some VCRs. Audio dub allows you to replace the audio of a videotape without changing the video.

Here's how to use it:

1. After you finish recording your random clips of students interacting, simply leave the tape in the video camera and rewind it.

2. Play the tape in the camera, and at the point you want to begin replacing the original sound with your new commentary, press pause.

3. Plug your microphone into the camera's microphone input jack (this will be a minijack on all consumer cameras).

4. Activate the audio dub feature on the camera. Check the owner's manual for simple instructions on how to do this. It usually involves a profound statement, like "To activate the audio dub mode, press the audio dub button while the tape is in the playback pause mode."

Now you're set. When you press the pause button to begin video playback, the audio dub light will remain lit—this indicates that sound is being recorded from the microphone and is replacing the original sound. But be warned: Using this approach forever erases your original sound. Thankfully, some VCRs offer audio dubbing—so you may first want to make a copy of your original footage, and then replace its sound. This will leave your original footage unchanged.

Person-on-the-Street Survey

Dress up as a stereotypical reporter (think Clark Kent) and hit the streets. Boldly approach strangers and ask them random, nonsensical, quirky questions. Video six or seven of these, and you have yourself a very humorous video.

- What would a chair look like if your knees bent the other way?
- Where do Club Med lifeguards go to get away from it all?
- Is there another word for "synonym"?
- Would a fly without wings be a walk?
- Can vegetarians eat animal crackers?
- If a turtle doesn't have a shell, is he homeless or naked?
- What do you do when you see an endangered species eating an endangered plant?
- Does the Little Mermaid wear an "algebra"?
- What was the best thing before sliced bread?
- If one synchronized swimmer drowns, do the rest drown, too?
- Is it true that cannibals don't eat clowns because they taste funny?
- Why is the alphabet in that order? Is it because of the song?
- Why is there an expiration date on sour cream?

Plant variation. Get someone unknown to the kids who'll be watching the video to play a "man on the street" that you'll be interviewing. You and the plant will agree on humorous answers ahead of time. For example, ask a plant about the upcoming football game between two rival high schools. He or she should respond in a way that surprises the kids or makes 'em laugh. Here are some examples:

- Kennedy plays Johnson tonight. Who do you think is going to win? *Answer:* Kennedy will win because their cheerleaders learned some new stunts from Mrs. Smith, one of the youth group volunteers.
- Should the kids at Wesley Church go to summer camp this year? *Answer:* Totally! Camp will be awesome! They're planning a killer bonfire on Thursday with tons of banana splits, Jars of Clay is doing a concert on the last night, and Hank Jones, our youth leader, might ask his girlfriend to marry him. Don't miss it!
- What do you think about Mike and Susie, two of our youth leaders at Calvary Church? *Answer:* They make the cutest couple! In fact, I heard Susie makes the best taco salad, and it drives Mike crazy when he eats it. And rumor has it that right now, as we're speaking, Mike is about to propose to Susie!
- Mark Smith wants to go to State U. What do you think his chances are? *Answer:* Hey, Mark's chances are great since he just got that full scholarship!

Video Dictionary

Ask people to define words you give them. These words can be particular to your group, relevant to your meeting or lesson, obscure words for everyday meanings, teenage slang, et cetera. Or get your hands on a dictionary of strange or funny words or phrases. The Internet has a lot of these. For example, "gorilla" can be defined as "how you prepare a cheese sandwich—you 'gorilla' it in the pan." The word "gruesome" could be defined as "what a little Jimmy did last year—he gruesome.'" (Okay, they can be cheesy, we admit! But fun!) Be sure to define the word and then use it in a sentence.

Not-So-Live Video

Tell kids that you're going to show them a live videoconference or interview. Then you (apparently) go live to another town, state, country, planet, whatever. You ask questions, the interviewee responds.

Of course, it's just a prerecorded video you made and rehearsed carefully to get the timing down between the questions and answers. As the video comes up, you have supposedly transmitted a live video to the person you are interviewing. This is great to do when a pastor or youth leader has gone out of town on vacation or whatever—just record the video footage before they leave.

Camcorder "Bests"

Students showcase their best burp, best joke, best scream, and so on, while being videotaped. Then show the tape to the group, vote for the winner, and give her a mock award.

Also try Best Gurbs, a "gurb" simply being a funny face that kids make for the camcorder. After watching five minutes of students "gurbing" for the camera, you'll be surprised (and sick, perhaps) at how some kids can contort their faces.

Happy Birthday Song

There are several ways to do this one. A favorite is to assign individual words in the "Happy Birthday" song to different people, videotape them singing their one word to the camera—and when you're done, you've got the entire song, sung word by word, each word by different people.

• Have someone sing each of the different stanzas and link them together into the video, verse by verse.
• Sing it in a foreign language, or several languages if you have the people.
• Sing at an extremely high pitch.
• Sing way too fast.
• Sing way too slow.
• Sing as if you're underwater; place your finger across your lips and "strum" your lips to make the bubbling sound.
• Sing as if very thirsty.
• Sing as if you're members of the Mafia.

Bus Roll

Try this next time you're on a van or bus trip. Explain to everyone exactly what you're going to do and assign roles. Then take the video camera to the front of the bus and begin taping.

After a moment, have a kid sitting toward the front of the bus stand up and scream, "Oh no! Look out!" At that point the kids begin to scream and jump up and down while they throw their hands straight up into the air. Then they throw their towels, shirts, backpacks, and everything else up in the air. Meanwhile, you're carefully rotating the camera around in circles several times, giving the illusion that the bus is rolling. After four or five rolls, steady the camera and have the kids stop jumping. By the end of the clip, they should all be "thrown" about the bus, on top of each other, in disarray—but safe and sound!

Big Splat
An effects video. Buy a large sheet of Plexiglas from a hardware store. Situate the camcorder behind the Plexiglas then throw things at the front of it—eggs, overripe fruit, yogurt, spaghetti, whatever. The effect is, uhh, eclectic. Yeah, that's it. Or use this technique when your video script calls for anything to be thrown. The perspective is particularly impressive.

Videograms
Like telegrams—appropriate for goodbyes, welcome homes, get wells, and other special occasions. Especially effective when sent to a person who's out of town or gone for some reason or another.

Describe Your First Kiss
The classic switcheroo! Videotape lots of brief clips of teenagers answering your question, "What does it feel like to throw up?" Then, at the meeting or event where you play back the tape, introduce it like this: "I recently asked a lot of your peers to describe their first kiss." Then roll the tape.

Bathroom variation. Videotape kid-on-the-street responses to your question, "Describe the stench in your bathroom immediately after someone else in your family has used it." Then introduce the playback with, "We asked a few people to describe Pastor Jim's sermons..."

Mad Libs variation. Kids answer some seemingly normal questions while you innocently capture their up-close, in-their-face answers on video. When you edit the tape, you turn diabolical and mismatch questions and answers.

Stupid Human Tricks

David Letterman has proved to the world that people will voluntarily do just about anything while a camera is pointed at them. Videotape the bizarre talents of your own students.

Make a Movie

This requires a little more work and planning. But if you have the time (yeah, right!), plan some time when you can actually make a movie. Have the kids help you to create a plot, place, conflict, and other plot elements. Then put the entire movie together. I aim for about a 30-minute movie. After you've completed the project, invite the rest of the kids over to watch "one of the great movies of our time." Oh...and here are a few tips to smooth the shooting process:

Plan a day when the kids can get together for at least a couple of hours to put this movie together.

Beforehand, or with the group, write a script. Group dynamics seem to make the creative process better, but the process also takes more time. Basically, you need a beginning, middle, and an end. You don't need all the details, just a basic idea of where the story is going.

Assign parts.

Gather costumes. They don't have to be expensive or elaborate, but they can really make a movie.

Begin shooting!

Some Ideas for a Movie...

• A Western with a villain, a heroine, and a hero. Basic plot. Villain hurts the heroine in some way, hero steps in to save the day.

• A scary, dramatic thriller with a person/group terrorized by a monster (or whatever). You could show the monster scaring different members of the group. Finally the group kills (or stops, or tames) the monster.

Here's a plot outline for a hero Joel created called the Buckethead Guy. He was like Superman or Batman. The plot was simple: The police chief receives a phone call that a criminal has escaped from prison. If you did a movie like this, you'd need to make up a bad guy, such as "Garbage Bag Man" or some nutty character like that. The superhero puts down the phone and exclaims, "The Garbage Bag Man is loose! I'll have to hunt him down and return him to prison where he belongs!"

Then a roving reporter interviews people on the street. Dress up members of your group and ask them what they think about the Garbage Bag Man being on the loose. Come up with goofy responses your kids will appreciate.

Next, create a scene in which the superhero meets the villain and they have it out. Then have a phone conversation between the police chief and the superhero, with the superhero saying, "All is safe now that Garbage Bag Man is in jail."

Now show new interviews with the same people on the streets for their responses. End with a witty closing remark by the superhero!

Skits on Tape
Just about any favorite skit of your group is doubly entertaining when videotaped and played back for the entire group. For a couple of classics to get you started, refer to the reproducible sketches on pages 156-159.

Starlit Theater
Whatever production your student video team has created, show it outside on a summer evening—in the church parking lot, a student's backyard, et cetera. You'll need a video projector, sound system and screen (or white wall). Serve hotdogs, popcorn, drinks, and enjoy the night.

Mr. or Ms. Curious
In the tradition of David Letterman, "Mr./Ms Curious" is an on-the-street video sketch template where you or a student, as Mr./Ms. Curious, has a license to be, well, curious about everything. An ace in the hole when you need a good, quick, and funny video sketch. Soon, though, "Mr./Ms. Curious" will become one of yours and your students' favorite sketches. The format is the same for each sketch: Mr./Ms. Curious (a very non-shy, Type-A teenager or volunteer) annoyingly probes, investigates, and explores whatever it is you want him to check out.

Examples:

Mr./Ms. Curious in the Great Outdoors. Mr./Ms. Curious gets curious about a neighborhood, street names, schools, beaches, mountains, et cetera. It's simply an opportunity to humorously explore a familiar or quirky landmark or otherwise distinctive feature of your town or area.

Mr./Ms. Curious at Your Workplace. Mr./Ms. Curious visits your kids when they're at their jobs and interviews their bosses and coworkers. Mr./Ms. Curious discovers where they take breaks, how much food they eat while on breaks, which coworker they have a crush on, and so on.

Mr./Ms. Curious with Your Parents. Mr./Ms. Curious visits and interviews parents of kids in your group. Your kids will be squirming in their pants wondering if their parents are next! Ask the parents various questions about their children, such as:
- What is the most embarrassing thing your child has ever done?
- What is the strangest thing he/she has ever eaten?
- What is the funniest thing he/she has ever done?
- Did he/she have any strange habits or practices as a young child?
- How did he/she eat when he/she was younger?
- Who was her/his first boyfriend or girlfriend?
- Was it hard potty-training him/her?

Mr./Ms. Curious at the Mall. Take Mr./Ms. Curious to the mall where he investigates what people are doing and buying. Ask strangers questions about what they bought that day. Ask to check out their bags. Ask why they bought what they did, and why they went to the particular store they went to. (You may want to check with mall security before commencing.)

A Day in the Life
You'll have endless ideas with this theme. Here are some ideas to get you started with your own wild-and-crazy "day in the life!"

A Day in the Life of a Youth Director. A spoof of a "typical" day in your life. The camcorder follows you around, recording your daily tasks: Work out, eat a good breakfast, read a book, et cetera—all acted in a humorous way (like bench-pressing a 100-pound middle schooler, a breakfast of pickles and a brownie, reading a Dr. Seuss book or a Tom Clancy novel as inspiration for next weekend's retreat). You get the idea. Exaggerate the misconceptions kids have about your typical day. (You may want to keep the tape out of the hands of the deacon or elder board, however!)

A Day in the Life of Sparky the Dog. Be sure to shoot this at dog-eye level, from its perspective. You may also want to add some shots of an actual dog doing actual things. Its day will consist of eating, napping, begging, doing tricks, chasing a stick, wrestling with its human master, and so on. Maybe end with a heroic achievement of the dog—saving its human from drowning, a carjacking, or some similar tragedy.

A Day in the Life of a Parent. Grab a crazy mom or dad who's willing to take a few hours to create this video with you. The typical day might include dragging her kids out of bed feet-first, getting fired from work, driving terribly, to name a few things. Recruit a parent whose child won't die of embarrassment.

How To

Another theme with endless possibilities! Try these on for size. Play with the idea. Have a pizza night just to brainstorm ideas with your kids.

How to Be Cool. In the opening of the video, say something like "WYTH-TV is proud to present the after-school documentary 'How to Be Cool,' starring Dr. Ima Dork." Dr. Dork comes out and talks for a few moments about his groundbreaking work as a cool teenager. Then go to a few video testimonials from characters that have benefited from Dr. Dork's work—these actors should really ham it up. Then on to the seven points of "How to Be Cool"—or three points, or however many you want to think up. They could include—

• Never pick your nose in public (and a video clip, of course, shows just this).

• Never wear pants five sizes too big (record examples of this).
• Never dance weird (record many examples of this).
Finally, cut to Dr. Dork again, and conclude the video.

How to Handle a Crisis. Choose several outlandish, humorous crises to cope with. These should be crises that are obviously exaggerated—say, the ripping off of someone's arm. Set up the scene—a card game, for instance—during which accusations of cheating are made, tempers flare, and an arm is pulled off. (Umm, make sure it's a fake arm, 'kay?) Then come the bogus steps to follow in handling this crisis (i.e., "Don't panic—call 911!"), all of it exaggerated and served up with a big helping of farce.

How to Eat a Possum. Or "How to Prepare Roadkill." Not popular with squeamish audiences, but it can be a hoot. Steps can include—
1. Place possum in microwave, being careful to arrange body around the center of the dish.
2. Chill the cooked possum in the freezer for 30 minutes.
3. Before warming up the possum, preheat oven to...

How to Babysit. Lots of potential here—before-and-after interviews with babysitters, interviews with little kids they babysat, lots of supposed rules to follow ("Never rent scary movies," for example), tips and techniques and more.

Mock commercials
As you watch TV programs and commercials, keep an eye open for ways to translate them into video ideas. In addition to the ideas below, you can make shaving-cream commercials, bug-killer commercials, cereal commercials—you name it. In this day of infomercials and shopping channels, there's no reason to keep your video to just 60 seconds. Use these commercials as, well, commercials within longer videos you've made.

M&Ms. Teenager actor dressed as little child, in a sparkling white shirt, appears eating M&Ms. Voiceover says, "M&M chocolate candies melt in your mouth, not in your hands." With that, the "child" opens her hands, smiles pretty. After a few seconds, chocolate—a lot of it—gushes out of her mouth and down her clean shirt.

Dog Food. Peel off a canned dog food label, and glue it on a can of corn beef hash. The announcer in this ad pitches the dog food—while the camcorder does a close-up on the label—opens the can, and begins eating it.

Smokeless Tobacco. Buy a can of smokeless tobacco, flush the 'baccy, and replace it with a couple of mashed Oreo cookies—just remember to lick the frosting off before you crumble them. Then have an all-sweetness-innocence-and-light middle school girl pitch an ad for smokeless tobacco. What viewers see her put in her mouth should stay there long enough to look like the real thing when, at the end of the commercial, she says, "Just a pinch between my cheek and gum gives me all day long satisfaction" and spits.

Mall Madness
There are a ton of things you can do with a camcorder at a mall. Just stay in control, because security guards tend not be crazy about roving pods of non-shopping kids in malls, so be careful. (Of course if you get questioned by security, record that, too!)

Phony Money. A classic. Tear off the corner of a $20 bill and tape it to the back of a bank deposit slip so that the corner of the bill peeks over and is visible behind the deposit slip. Place it strategically on the mall floor, where people will walk by and notice it. Videotape their reaction when they realize they've been fooled.
Coin variation. From a magic or hobby shop, buy a large coin with super-strong tape on its back (they do sell them!). Tape the coin to the floor in the mall, then videotape people as they walk by and do everything they can to pick up the coin, try to kick it, and so on. What often makes the best footage is their reaction when they realize they've been had.

Store Manager Interviews. Have kids interview store managers. Something that makes it even more fun is to allow managers to preview the questions and come up with their own

responses. For example, if you ask, "Is Susie friendly with cus- tomers?" the store manager could reply, "Oh, yes. She's very friendly, especially to the guy customers. When this one guy came in..."
- How long has this person been working here?
- Is he/she a good worker?
- How would you describe this person's work ethic?
- Does this person seem flirtatious with customers?
- How would you describe this person's attitude about being at work here?
- Does this person have any annoying habits you've noticed?

Food Court Conversations. At lunchtime take your cam- corder to a mall's food court, and with the strangers' permis- sion, sit down with them and interview them while they lunch. (You may find that teenagers and senior citizens make the best interviewees under such circumstances.) Ask them about their food, eating habits, et cetera. Sample their food and drink, if it's appropriate. You can set up a lot of things off-camera to make what is on camera hilarious.

Resources from Youth Specialties

Ideas Library

Ideas Library on CD-ROM 2.0
Administration, Publicity, & Fundraising
Camps, Retreats, Missions, & Service Ideas
Creative Meetings, Bible Lessons, & Worship Ideas
Crowd Breakers & Mixers
Discussion & Lesson Starters
Discussion & Lesson Starters 2
Drama, Skits, & Sketches
Drama, Skits, & Sketches 2
Drama, Skits, & Sketches 3
Games
Games 2
Games 3
Holiday Ideas
Special Events

Bible Curricula

Creative Bible Lessons from the Old Testament
Creative Bible Lessons in 1 & 2 Corinthians
Creative Bible Lessons in Galatians and Philippians
Creative Bible Lessons in John
Creative Bible Lessons in Romans
Creative Bible Lessons on the Life of Christ
Creative Bible Lessons in Psalms
Downloading the Bible Kit
Wild Truth Bible Lessons
Wild Truth Bible Lessons 2
Wild Truth Bible Lessons—Pictures of God
Wild Truth Bible Lessons—Pictures of God 2

Topical Curricula

Creative Junior High Programs from A to Z, Vol. 1 (A-M)
Creative Junior High Programs from A to Z, Vol. 2 (N-Z)
Girls: 10 Gutsy, God-Centered Sessions on Issues That Matter to Girls
Guys: 10 Fearless, Faith-Focused Sessions on Issues That Matter to Guys
Good Sex
Live the Life! Student Evangelism Training Kit
The Next Level Youth Leader's Kit
Roaring Lambs
So What Am I Gonna Do with My Life?
Student Leadership Training Manual
Student Underground
Talking the Walk

What Would Jesus Do? Youth Leader's Kit
Wild Truth Bible Lessons
Wild Truth Bible Lessons 2
Wild Truth Bible Lessons—Pictures of God
Wild Truth Bible Lessons—Pictures of God 2

Discussion Starters

Discussion & Lesson Starters (Ideas Library)
Discussion & Lesson Starters 2 (Ideas Library)
EdgeTV
Every Picture Tells a Story
Get 'Em Talking
Keep 'Em Talking!
Good Sex Drama
Have You Ever...?
What If...?
Would You Rather...?
High School TalkSheets—Updated!
More High School TalkSheets—Updated!
High School TalkSheets from Psalms and Proverbs—Updated!
Junior High-Middle School TalkSheets—Updated!
More Junior High-Middle School TalkSheets—Updated!
Junior High-Middle School TalkSheets from Psalms and Proverbs—Updated!
Name Your Favorite
Real Kids Ultimate Discussion-Starting Videos:
      Castaways
      Growing Up Fast
      Hardship & Healing
      Quick Takes
      Survivors
      Word on the Street
Small Group Qs
Unfinished Sentences

Drama Resources

Drama, Skits, & Sketches (Ideas Library)
Drama, Skits, & Sketches 2 (Ideas Library)
Drama, Skits, & Sketches 3 (Ideas Library)
Dramatic Pauses
Good Sex Drama
Spontaneous Melodramas
Spontaneous Melodramas 2
Super Sketches for Youth Ministry

Game Resources

Games (Ideas Library)
Games 2 (Ideas Library)
Games 3 (Ideas Library)
Junior High Game Nights
More Junior High Game Nights
Play It!
Screen Play CD-ROM

Additional Programming Resources
(also see Discussion Starters*)*

Camps, Retreats, Missions, & Service Ideas (Ideas Library)
Creative Meetings, Bible Lessons, & Worship Ideas (Ideas Library)
Crowd Breakers & Mixers (Ideas Library)
Everyday Object Lessons
Great Fundraising Ideas for Youth Groups
More Great Fundraising Ideas for Youth Groups
Great Retreats for Youth Groups
Great Talk Outlines for Youth Ministry
Holiday Ideas (Ideas Library)
Incredible Questionnaires for Youth Ministry
Kickstarters
Memory Makers
Special Events (Ideas Library)
Videos That Teach
Videos That Teach 2
Worship Services for Youth Groups

Quick Question Books

Have You Ever...?
Name Your Favorite
Unfinished Sentences
What If...?
Would You Rather...?

Videos & Video Curricula

Dynamic Communicators Workshop
EdgeTV
Live the Life! Student Evangelism Training Kit
Make 'Em Laugh!
Purpose-Driven® Youth Ministry Training Kit

Real Kids Ultimate Discussion-Starting Videos:
    Castaways
    Growing Up Fast
    Hardship & Healing
    Quick Takes
    Survivors
    Word on the Street
Student Underground
Understanding Your Teenager Video Curriculum
Youth Ministry Outside the Lines

Especially for Junior High

Creative Junior High Programs from A to Z, Vol. 1 (A-M)
Creative Junior High Programs from A to Z, Vol. 2 (N-Z)
Junior High Game Nights
More Junior High Game Nights
Junior High-Middle School TalkSheets—Updated!
More Junior High-Middle School TalkSheets—Updated!
Junior High-Middle School TalkSheets from Psalms and Proverbs—Updated!
Wild Truth Journal for Junior Highers
Wild Truth Bible Lessons
Wild Truth Bible Lessons 2
Wild Truth Journal—Pictures of God
Wild Truth Bible Lessons—Pictures of God

Student Resources

Downloading the Bible: A Rough Guide to the New Testament
Downloading the Bible: A Rough Guide to the Old Testament
Grow for It! Journal through the Scriptures
So What Am I Gonna Do with My Life?
Spiritual Challenge Journal: The Next Level
Teen Devotional Bible
What (Almost) Nobody Will Tell You about Sex
What Would Jesus Do? Spiritual Challenge Journal

Clip Art

Youth Group Activities (print)
Clip Art Library Version 2.0 (CD-ROM)

Digital Resources

Clip Art Library Version 2.0 (CD-ROM)
Great Talk Outlines for Youth Ministry
Hot Illustrations CD-ROM
Ideas Library on CD-ROM 2.0
Screen Play
Youth Ministry Management Tools

LINCOLN CHRISTIAN COLLEGE AND SEMINARY

Professional Resources

Administration, Publicity, & Fundraising (Ideas Library)
Dynamic Communicators Workshop
Great Talk Outlines for Youth Ministry
Help! I'm a Junior High Youth Worker!
Help! I'm a Small-Group Leader!
Help! I'm a Sunday School Teacher!
Help! I'm an Urban Youth Worker!
Help! I'm a Volunteer Youth Worker!
Hot Illustrations for Youth Talks
More Hot Illustrations for Youth Talks
Still More Hot Illustrations for Youth Talks
Hot Illustrations for Youth Talks 4
How to Expand Your Youth Ministry
How to Speak to Youth...and Keep Them Awake at the Same Time
Junior High Ministry (Updated & Expanded)
Just Shoot Me: A Practical Guide for Using Your Video Camera in Youth
    Ministry
Make 'Em Laugh!
The Ministry of Nurture
Postmodern Youth Ministry
Purpose-Driven® Youth Ministry
Purpose-Driven® Youth Ministry Training Kit
So *That's* Why I Keep Doing This!
Teaching the Bible Creatively
A Youth Ministry Crash Course
Youth Ministry Management Tools
The Youth Worker's Handbook to Family Ministry

Academic Resources

Four Views of Youth Ministry & the Church
Starting Right
Youth Ministry That Transforms